Caryn Franklin has worked in the fashion industry for fifteen years. Starting at *i-D Magazine* in the early eighties, she stayed for six years to become the first fashion editor and later a co-editor. She has always enjoyed the challenge of television, and researched and presented for a variety of programmes, including cable television's *Music Box* and Channel 4's premier fashion programme, *Swank*, which was transmitted in 1984. She was also the first fashion editor to co-produce a small series of fashion videos for Channel 4's Network Seven. Nearly ten years ago Caryn began co-presenting the BBC's *Clothes Show* and has also written and directed for the programme. Her passionate interests are the nature of fashion and its manipulation of femininity. But as well as initiating features around the above, she enjoys reporting from the frontlines of the fashion capitals come showtime, and has contributed her knowledge to a variety of other television and radio programmes. She has always remained firmly grounded in the fashion industry and is a part-time lecturer in media studies and fashion communications, as well as an external examiner to a variety of colleges.

Inspired by her sister's own battle with anorexia some years ago, Caryn spends time visiting schools to talk about eating disorders and the fashion industry's preoccupation with thinness.

Niall McInerney has been a freelance catwalk photographer for the past 20 years — travelling between London, Milan, Paris, New York and beyond — working for numerous magazines and newspapers. He has an extraordinary collection of over 10 million slides.

franklin on fashion

by caryn franklin

with photographs by Niall McInerney

An Imprint of HarperCollins*Publishers*

Pandora

An Imprint of HarperCollins*Publishers*

77–85 Fulham Palace Road

Hammersmith, London W6 8JB

1160 Battery Street

San Francisco, California 94111–1213

Published by Pandora 1996

10 9 8 7 6 5 4 3 2 1

© Caryn Franklin 1996

© Photographs by Niall McInerney 1996

Caryn Franklin asserts the moral right to

be identified as the author of this work

A catalogue record for this book

is available from the British Library

ISBN 0 04 440986 9

Printed in Great Britain by the Bath Press

To Mateda, a book on fashion and other f words.

Acknowledgements

First I would like to thank Rosemary Sandberg for her help in getting this project off the ground. As an agent her support has been invaluable. To Georgina Goodman my special thanks. Having just finished a book together, I thought she'd throw up her hands at the idea of another one so soon, but to my delight, she was there with her constant support and superior researching skills. Thank you to Suzanne Marston, Juliet Yashar and Tracey Sawyer, for extra research and opinions. For specialist information I thank Sarah Doukas of Storm Modelling Agency; Elaine Kirschel, cosmetic scientist; Robbin Derrick, Art Director of *Vogue* magazine; Matthew Jet of Promostyle; beauty editor Anna-Marie Solowij; Rob Harrison of *Ethical Consumer* magazine; Simon Ward at the British Fashion Council; Suzannah Handley at the Royal College of Art; Kate T. Fletcher at the Surrey Institute of Art and Design; and TMS Partnership for data supplied on jeans sales figures.

I would also like to thank the Pandora dream team, especially Belinda Budge for her interest in this book and Sara Dunn, whose encouragement and clear view have been invaluable. Thank you to Niall McInerney for his wonderful library of fashion moments on film and Sally Dawson and Derren Gilhooley for their patient assistance with picture research. Thank you fashion historians Colin McDowell and Georgina O'Hara and anthropologist/psychologist John Liggett, whose writings have educated me over the years. Thanks to Ian Denyer for love and support at 60,000. And to Urban Species on the CD player, thanks for the soundtrack. At last, 'Light at the end of the tunnel.'

introduction

When I worked at *i-D Magazine* I was catering to a

small group of discerning punters. Fashion was a pair

of Dr Marten boots and a tutu (for me at least) and

clothes were bought second hand or made. In the early

eighties there were no supermodels and catwalk shows

were shrouded in secrecy. Times have changed.

Today the image of Kate Moss or Christy Turlington

can be seen on every corner and the cult of the label

continues to grow. Women especially are dedicated

consumers. In Britain we spend an annual £14 billion on

clothes alone, double the expenditure of men. But we

don't just buy the product. We buy the lifestyle and the message or party line from the designer. He or she will employ an advertising agency to spread the word, either inviting us to join this special club or implicitly refusing entry. If we feel like outsiders, perhaps we'll spend more to achieve acceptance. Women of larger sizes know all about this particular strategy.

Fashion, on one level or another, infiltrates the daily lives of us all, and since beginning work in this industry, I have come to appreciate the excitement and energy it creates as well as the power generated by the accompanying seductive imagery. Of course this book takes a look at that world full of glamour, beauty and allure. But it is a selective sweep across a huge terrain, punctuated by coverage of topics I'm often asked to

talk about by *Clothes Show* viewers. I have also saved

space for designer info and the history of our clothes

and appearance, as well as the evolution of the fashion

industry we know today.

Naturally I include my own opinions concerning what

is on offer from the fashion world, with no apologies for

an occasional intolerance of this glorious luvvie-land.

You can read from start to finish or use the A–Z format

(words in bold highlight other entries) to follow the

subjects you wish to know more about.

adornment An activity as old as civilization itself. In ancient times, we simply decorated our skins with vegetable dyes, tattoos or scarification, and hung brightly-coloured objects or valued possessions on our bodies. The development of **clothes** and the creation of fashion has seen the basic need to beautify turned into a multi-billion dollar industry.

advertising Advertisers have spent a fortune perfecting the art of selling us products we don't need, by appealing to our insecurities. For women, these can be many, since this culture often encourages us to be dissatisfied with our bodies from an early **age**. The fashion industry requires us to buy what it sells

A is for Adornment. French designer Jean-Paul Gaultier celebrates African Tribal body adornment in his Sring/Summer collection of '94 twice a year at the very least; once for Spring/Summer and once for Autumn/ Winter. Although many of us may feel we have perfectly serviceable **clothes** in our wardrobes from past seasons, all fashion advertising suggests that we can be new and improved, happier, more successful, more attractive and more loved, if we just acquired this latest product.

Advertising imagery also sends other messages. For the majority of women, the long-legged, lean-hipped, fresh-faced, pale-skinned professional **models** featured in most advertising campaigns, serve as role models never to be successfully copied; a sense of perpetual anxiety is nurtured and encouraged. **Beauty** advertising is particularly adept at exploiting the fears of older women. Many ads aimed at those over thirty feature portraits of young women considerably under thirty, with no signs of wrinkles or ageing skin. When campaigns do use photographs of seasoned models, it is only after their complexions have been airbrushed to remove wrinkles. Italian actress and Lancôme house model Isabella Rossellini was dismissed shortly before her fortieth birthday, but reinstated after public outcry. She continues to model, but only after her **face** has been thoroughly touched-up and all signs of natural ageing removed by computer technology.

a 2

africa European fashion has always looked to Africa, but since few African **fashion designers** or **textile designers** have access to the western fashion industry themselves, the designs we see are big-name design houses' ideas of Africa; a seasonal fantasy of bright colour, exhilarating textile prints and appropriately themed **hair** and **make-up** styles. The modern European fashion industry's attraction to Africa began when the American **Josephine Baker** arrived in Paris in 1925; her extraordinary style and charisma single-handedly aroused a mainstream interest in African culture. Today, the European fashion industry handles Africa like a holiday village to be visited when respite from uptight city life and restrictive winter styles are needed. 'Wish you were here' **fashion shoots** become our experience of Africa, a faraway land of plush sensuality and welcoming exotica. In the **magazine** world, images of **black models** tend to depict them as smouldering temptresses. Natural hairstyles of tight curls, braiding or locks are tolerated briefly as part of the look, but when the **fashion shoot** is over, most black models must put on their **wigs** for commercial employment.

afro The Afro hairstyle enjoyed major popularity during the seventies, and was wonderfully sported by civil rights activist Angela Davis. 'Big hair' was about African/American men and women proclaiming a political presence, and highlighting a movement which demanded basic civil rights. It was developed as a reaction to the crude bleaching and straightening processes adopted by many black people under pressure to fit white western ideals. The Afro evoked an almost mythological image of **Africa**, where **hair** was natural and free. In fact the Afro took large amounts of manicuring to get the look just right, and those in Africa who did sport it tended to be the rich élite copying the latest styles from America. When punks adopted big hair, along with other motifs borrowed from African culture, they could only achieve the high-rise hair effect with the aid of soap, or sugar mixed with water, or for the extremely zealous, glue.

age The fashion and **beauty** industries have little to say about the positive effects of getting older and wiser. Age is sold to us as a predicament to be avoided or at least postponed. Age is physical deterioration alone, and for a woman, akin to a social misdemeanour.

alaia, azzedine The **supermodel** choice as a designer of slinky figure-hugging **clothes**, many top **models** have preferred payment in kind rather than cash. He is best known for his striking black fitted designs, which at the height of the body-conscious eighties featured in **magazines** worldwide. Born in Tunisia, Alaia received rave reviews for creating the sexiest clothes in **Paris**; the result of a lifetime obsession with French elegance. Reared on fine art and *Vogue* magazine, apart from short stints for design houses (he cut patterns for **Dior** for five days) he is self-taught. Relatively unknown until the eighties, having worked out of his apartment and operating as an au pair and sometimes a housekeeper, he made his mark at his first show in **New York**, recreating the hourglass look in softly draped jersey. For Alaia there is only one kind of woman, the others are invisible. 'When a woman does not want to be noticed she should put on a veil, or she should stay at home with a cup of tea and wait for the moment to pass.'

armani, giorgio

Known as the man who turned understatement into an art form. In **Milan** he is treated with much reverence and does not show in the standard venue. Instead, fashion press are invited to pre-**show** cocktails in his own theatre with built-in catwalk. There follows a signature presentation featuring subtly-dressed **models** alighting at one end of the runway, and magically disappearing at t'other end in wave after wave of coordinated pastel designs. So devoted are his followers, that Mr Armani recently received a rapturous ovation when his lighting system failed mid-show. Armani does not use **supermodels**, preferring instead to pair his **clothes** with the serene **beauty** of lesser-known women. The real star of the show then takes the final curtain call with a carefully staged finale, underlining his god-like presence as he stretches out his arms to his disciples.

Born just outside Milan in 1935, Giorgio suffered recurring nightmares as a result of an incident with a wartime grenade. He studied medicine at Milan University but decided he couldn't cope with the sight of blood, and after military service he began work as a window-dresser for an Italian chain store. In 1961 he began work with **menswear** designer Nino Cerruti. In 1975 he set up his own company and began designing menswear that subtly challenged traditional shapes by removing the stuffing, stiffening, lining and stitching to produce the deconstructed jacket.

Meanwhile his womenswear appropriated masculine tailoring touches to create a sophisticated cool, and he became the designer of choice for a host of discerning female stars, from Jodie Foster to **Cindy Crawford**. He is known as the 'jacket and pants king', a label he would prefer to lose. Rumours abound that he insists on regulation uniforms for staff, together with scrubbed faces and no nail varnish, that the hangers in his shops must be a precise width apart, that he wraps all the cutlery in his kitchen in plastic, and that he even shakes hands with gloves on. I can vouch that this last one at least is untrue!

Armaní was the first to explore diffusion concepts, diluting the design and extravagant manufacture to offer **clothes** and accessories to a wider audience for less money. His empire is worth £400 million. At sixty he announced that he would continue for ten years and no more. Although he is depicted as a joyless workaholic, Mr Armani is not without a sense of humour. In his office, he displays a large painting of certain fashion dignitaries; included is **Karl Lagerfeld**, in a one-piece swimming costume with **Chanel** handcuffs at his feet. I think that says it all.

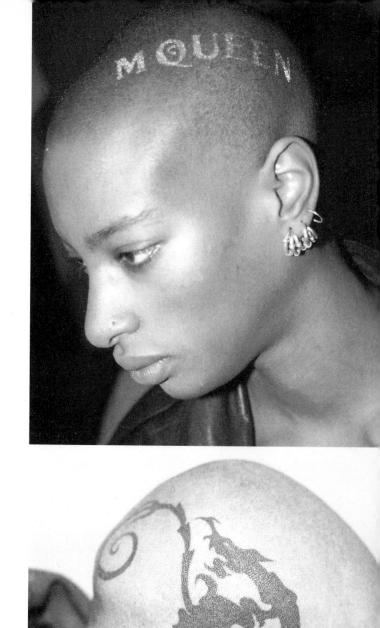

baby doll A look that surfaces every now and then, mixing the sexually knowing woman with child-like **clothes** and poses. Begun in the sixties, and spearheaded by Twiggy, whose bottom was permanently on display beneath the short skirts or girlie shifts she modelled. The look was resurrected in the early nineties on the catwalks of **Milan**, particularly by **Dolce & Gabbana**, and **Gianni Versace**. There are also women who celebrate this style – christened by Mr Versace as *Kinderwhore* – either by their wearing it, like Courtney Pine, or designing it, like Anna Sui. Courtney and Anna both have a liking for a babyish femininity, accessorizing the look with all manor of cutie extras like pink ribbons, bows, tummies on show and even knickers.

B is for Bald. More and more women choose to shave off their hair. Catwalk models have helped pioneer the trend.

This unappealing look surfaces at periods in history when the sex wars are at their height. In Twiggy's generation, the advent of the pill and the Women's Liberation Movement gave women a newly acquired control of their own sexual destiny; and the nineties have come to signify a time of disruption and adjustment around fast-changing gender roles. In these confusing periods for men, how helpful that women dress up like toddlers, pretending to be just little girls at heart.

baker, josephine

The first **supermodel**. Josephine Baker was born in 1906 in Missouri, in the southern US, and left home at sixteen to join a touring dancing group. She found work in the choruses of Boston and Broadway, and then joined the Revue Negre, travelling to **London** and **Paris**. She launched herself in Paris from the Folies Bergère and the Casino de Paris, where her first performance wearing black **lipstick**, slicked **hair** and a skirt of real banana skins caused a sensation. Traditional stage **make-up** at this time was burned cork ashes and chalky, pale lips (worn by both black and white performers). Baker's new style was universally copied, and she was credited as being one of the most beautiful women the modern world had seen. She often appeared scantily clad, immaculately accessorized with necklets, bracelets, anklets, brightly-dyed gloves and feathers, with her skin gleaming and oiled, and was pursued by **fashion designers** and **fashion photographers**.

bald
Originally an African style, Caucasian women have also adopted the no-hair look with striking results. French model Eve rose to fame on the catwalk **modelling** for **Chanel**, with her shaved head and grey dragon tattoo. Female pop stars have also opted for a Bic razor as a comb replacement, and a generation of young women who followed suit challenged long-held traditions about femininity, **hair** and attractiveness.

After the last war, many French women had their heads forcibly shaved. Their baldness alerted others that they had been accused of betraying their country by falling in love or aiding enemy soldiers. The public removal of hair was punishment and humiliation; in this instance times really have changed.

barbie A plastic doll around nine inches high with exaggerated body proportions (scaled up she's 39–18–33), this strange toy has inspired international **fashion editors** to construct elaborate fashion spreads in celebration of her vacuous and manufactured looks. **Gianni Versace**, known for his extravagant designs and love of rock chic **glamour**, sent his **models** down the catwalk with **hair** and **make-up** copied to look like our airhead heroine. Some women even claim to have used Barbie as a role model for plastic surgery operations, while others pay hundreds of pounds for a 'box fresh' early model.

Every year Babs adds one hundred and fifty new outfits to her wardrobe, and unlike many a **supermodel**, is still going strong at thirty-seven. Such is her popularity that Mattel earn around £300 million worldwide by reinventing her every year. Barbie's sequined reign could shortly be over, however, as Feral Cheryl, a teenage doll from Down Under, complete with tattoos, unshaven legs, pierced nipples, dreadlocks and pubic hair, snatches the spotlight.

beauty All societies have had rigid definitions of what is beautiful and what isn't. For the Ancient Greeks beauty was about proportion, balance and symmetry, while medieval artists believed the perfect **face** was neatly divisible into sevenths; the shaven forehead and eyebrows popular among young English women in the twelfth century now look distinctly unattractive. The standards may change, but those who set them do not, they are exclusively masculine and Caucasian. As Charlotte Perkins Gilman wrote in 1911, 'Much of what man calls beauty in woman is not human beauty at all, but gross over-development of certain points which appeal to him as a male.'

Tests have shown repeatedly that beautiful people are treated with more tolerance, they are awarded better jobs and are even smiled at more often. **Models** in **magazines** laugh and the message is conveyed that beautiful people are happy people. And in Hollywood the highest female earners embody definitions of North American beauty – **blonde**, blue-eyed, slim and young. They seem to live exciting lives on and off screen, and as 'global royalty' they set fashion standards across the board.

Backstage before any catwalk **show**, beauty competitions take place. Women compete for the attention of the top hairdresser or **make-up** artist, leaving lesser known faces to the assistants. Being beautiful does not mean the competing is over; being ordinary does not exclude women from having to compete; and being young (as young as two), does not prohibit entry into the competition in the first place.

beauty without cruelty charity Set up in 1959 by

Lady Dowding to inform people about the suffering and exploitation of animals in the cosmetics industry, and to promote cruelty-free alternatives. Many cosmetics (the term includes not only **make-up** in general, but also **face** creams, **hair**, bath and nail products, deodorants, sunscreens, hair dyes, aftershaves, soap and toothpaste) still use some degree of animal testing. Even if a disclaimer appears on the side of the final product, the ingredients themselves may still have found their way into the bodies of animals incarcerated in small cages.

In addition, many ingredients derived from the animals themselves are used as by-products of the slaughterhouse. Due to a recent European Community Cosmetics Directive, toiletries and cosmetics will soon be forced to label ingredients in their products. Many suspect that descriptions of animal fats and placentas in soaps, face creams and commercial toothpastes will be enough to effect radical change. More cruelty-free products are becoming available, not just through mail order or health food shops, but also regular chemists and department stores. Funding for alternatives has come largely from the cosmetics industry itself, as increasing consumer pressure signals the demand for animal testing to stop.

belly button
The latest site for erotic focus and piercing operations. Hipsters are ideal accessories to navel jewellery.

black hair
The fashion circuit boasts of its quest for individuality and freedom; but Tyra Banks wears a long straight wig with **blonde** highlights for Swedish clients Hennes, and **Naomi Campbell** is rarely allowed out without her pretend western hair-do. In America, black girls between the ages of six and twelve can buy a children's formula relaxer kit. They do so in their millions, using the powerful chemicals on their young scalps to remove the natural curl. On the front cover of *Ebony* **magazine**, fifty years of fashion and **beauty** is celebrated with pictures of five beautiful women, all of whom have western hairstyles.

Black hairstyles are innovative and ornate. Women wear highly-styled sculptural mountains of weave, braiding and synthetic hair, while some men choose to shave works of art onto their heads. In the real world, Caucasian boys and girls, influenced by musical role models, copy what they see. Even traditional styles like locks, plaits and cornrows have inspired generations of non-Africans. In the early eighties hairdresser Simon Forbes marketed the 'white rasta' look with hair extensions from his popular Kensington salon Antenna.

black models
Lorraine Pascal advertises Häagen Dazs, Veronica Webb fronts a Revlon campaign and Naomi and Tyra are two of the best known faces in the **modelling** world. But it is only recently that black mannequins have begun to appear in shop windows, and mainstream **make-up** companies have developed products for African and Asian skins. In a culture that still labels pale tights as

'flesh' or 'nude', and operates racist policies where cover girls are concerned, there is still considerable ground to cover. Models can be told they are 'too dark', or not 'black enough', by Caucasian clients who have a fixed idea of what black **beauty** should be. In the fifties only a few black models were able to find work; Dorothea Towles became the first black model to work for top designers in Paris. In the sixties Broadway stars like Marsha Hunt of the musical *Hair* and Diana Ross forged careers and a presence in mainstream America. Beverly Johnson was much in demand on international catwalks, and she was also the first black model to appear on the cover of American *Vogue*, in 1974. She has since appeared on a further five hundred covers, and along with her contemporaries Pat Cleveland and Iman (now Mrs David Bowie) has spread a vision of black beauty beyond minority communities. In 1983 Vanessa Williams became the first black woman to win the Miss America pageant. In the nineties two black women simultaneously held both the Miss America and Miss USA titles. Great Britain, however, has yet to offer an equivalent. Advertisers who do not use black models insist that Caucasian consumers do not respond to black role models. Strange, then, that such celebrated Caucasian women as Madonna seek silicone lip implants and tan or curl up their hair tightly, thereby emulating natural African features.

blonde Every woman's desire, as the ad campaigns would have us believe.

Linda Evangelista was seen to attain **supermodel** status and international fame almost overnight when hairdresser Sam McNight cut off her **brunette** tresses and dyed the remainder platinum. Linda was treading a well-worn path, which Twiggy and Marilyn Monroe, amongst others, had already trodden. Our fascination with blonde could date back to classical Roman times, when women, mostly dark haired, used dye or bleach to achieve a degree of blonde exotica amongst their contemporaries. Angels in Christian heaven are frequently depicted as blonde, as are cherubic babies. For starlets like Alice (in Wonderland), Goldilocks, Rapunzel and Cinderella, long blonde ringlets are *de rigueur*. Blondes, although awarded the cultural seal of approval in terms of desirability, have difficulty being taken seriously. 'Bubbly', 'bombshell' and 'dumb' are adjectives suggesting a femininity that has no use for intellect.

bloomer, amelia jenks
Editor in the 1850s of the women's temperance and suffrage paper *The Lily*, Amelia Bloomer was a political activist and mother of a modern-day dress code which western women now take for granted.

The Bloomer costume was designed by Elizabeth Smith Miller (cousin of one of the founders of the women's movement in America). The all-in-one jacket, skirt and Turkish-style **trousers** gathered together at the ankles, formed a **uniform** specifically designed to allow freedom of movement. They were originally worn by Amelia Bloomer as part of a campaign which, as well as insisting on the right to vote, the right to education and the right to work, demanded a sensible dress code for women. By 1857 'Bloomer' had become a term of ridicule, as those threatened by the suffragette movement looked to humiliate its members. Wearers were forced to abandon their early attempt at practical dress in order to avoid further derision for the whole of the women's movement. To this day the use of the word 'bloomer' is linked with hilarity or stupidity.

body hair
The majority of women grow **hair** on their legs, underarms and faces, yet most are unwilling to allow it to stay. Shaving, tweezering, creaming and waxing are all employed to effect removal. Electrolysis completely eradicates hair follicles, rendering re-growth impossible. And all this because body hair is associated with a lack of femininity. In the nineteenth century medical men warned women that too much knowledge would render them infertile. Today, the advertising equivalent reminds us that no matter what we may achieve our first job is to be feminine, soft and hairless.

bottoms The introduction of **Alexander McQueen**'s low-cut tailored **trouser** inspired a selection of low-cut backless dresses and skirts from fellow **fashion designers**. Bottom cleavage was not a new concept; John Bates, an influential name in the sixties and seventies, made headlines with his daring designs and had also been responsible for the costumes of Emma Peel in *The Avengers*. Bottoms are a must if you want to sit comfortably, yet many western women spend a lifetime hating the soft mounds of flesh located at the top of their thighs. Other cultures are more hospitable; in Africa and the Caribbean, women are revered for their ample thighs and bottoms, and bony or boyish backsides are not considered attractive in any way.

B is for breasts. The fashion industry is besotted with bosoms. Designers explore a variety of design ideas to celebrate these fleshy orbs.

bras When lingerie giants Triumph employed Czech siren Eva Herzigova to fill out the Wonderbra campaign, a new objective in **underwear** marketing emerged – encouraging men's involvement in the selling of bras. Some local authorities worried that Ms H's piercing blue eyes and plush cleavage might cause traffic accidents as she and her **breasts** stared down from billboards with a welcoming 'hello boys'. Sales increased by a whopping 41 per cent and Eva went on to **supermodel** stardom. Now photographic luminaries like Herb Ritts construct erotic images of women in their smalls. Gossard's Glossies range of seamless bras features the copy line 'Who said a woman can't get pleasure from something soft?', and shows a reclining beauty in long grass waiting for something hard. We've come a long way from the original intentions of the brassiere.

The brassiere was allegedly invented in 1913 by American debutante Caress Crosby (this was not her real name, but full marks for early marketing flair), and began life as an insignificant little undergarment. It was intended to fetter the breasts of

western womankind at a time when dancing, increasingly more energetic, was giving rise to a certain amount of ungainly jiggling about. Comfort was the main concern at the time, and the garment looked like two triangular hankies sewn together, fastened at the back with cord. By the thirties luxury underwear was becoming big business.

Besides providing valuable support for an area of the female physique lacking in natural muscle, bras were to give everyone a lift. Stitched, padded and even inflated, bras lifted breasts upwards and outwards. By the fifties, bra shapes were conical and unnatural, complementing the **New Look**, and many women sewed buttons at the tips to further the point. Playtex delivered a 'lift and separate' promise during the sixties, that passed into copywriting mythology. In the seventies, 'cleavage' became the bra objective, by which point underwired, padded jobbies were offering up feminine wobbly bits for casual view and masculine response. Today's bra requires some twenty to thirty components to make up a complex piece of corsetry engineering. Bra adverts usually neglect to mention the comfort factor, preferring instead to invest this plucky little undergarment with the power to attract Mr Right.

breasts Varying enormously in size and shape, breasts are a part of the female anatomy that never escapes attention. Massively over-hyped by the fashion industry as beacons of femininity, they are marketed and re-marketed every season by **fashion designers** and **fashion editors** as body parts most essential to display or conceal. The external appearance is all-important, to the point where many women, including **models**, pay large amounts of money to cosmetic surgeons for silicone implants. Some figures indicate that one in forty US women have opted for this treatment, even though the procedure can be risky and sometimes even life-endangering. Newspapers, seasonal calendars, postcards, specialist 'breast and bottom' **magazines** and of course fashion **advertising** imagery are just a few places to spot the ubiquitous breast. But don't expect any variation in size or style; pert and youthful varieties, with nipples symmetrically located dead centre, are the only types on offer. **Fashion designers** frequently send out bare-breasted models in catwalk finales, while others make oversized statements about shape and appearance. **Jean-Paul Gaultier** constructed huge cone-like falsies on knitted dresses, while **Vivienne Westwood**, with the help of her boned and padded 'liberty bodice', preferred her breasts flattened and relocated somewhere under her chin.

british

British style is revered all over the world and British design creativity is regarded as second to none. But the British public is unimpressed. Designers like **Vivienne Westwood** have consistently endured ridicule from the British media. It seems most British women do not understand what she does, and British men are scornful. But other notions of British style are copied all over the world. Countries like Japan and North America buy into a perceived idea of what they think British style really is, and companies like Mulberry, Aquascutum and Burberry export a uniform of the country squire hinting at outdoor pursuits like hunting, shooting and fishing. It's a particularly blokey look, traditional, upright and earnest, reminiscent of the days of the Empire. The female equivalent of this attire is drab and completely lacking in individuality, almost like army uniform with gleaming buttons and natural colouring. The women's styles play a supportive role, lieutenant to the revved-up commanders of the male style.

brunette

Advertising has often used brown **hair** to suggest the presence of intelligence, adorning the **models** with bookish spectacles. Sometimes these girls were saddies looking for a bottle of something to lighten their boring brown tresses and pep up their social lives. The other stereotype sees brunettes as naughty, sometimes evil, never cute or fragile. Brunettes are rarely allowed a wholesome 'girl-next-door' sex appeal; theirs is a smouldering sexual allure, sometimes deviant, maybe dangerous. Brunettes will always be honourary baddies, until wicked **witches** are beautiful **blondes**.

campbell, naomi The British element – and possibly the most diverse performer of the international **supermodel** crew – Campbell is the only **black model** among the original group. She comes from Streatham in south **London**, and was quite literally spotted in Covent Garden as a student in 1986, shortly before her sixteenth birthday, by Elite Model Agency proprietor Beth Bolt. On her first **modelling** assignment, she exhibited a unique grace, and her camera skills soon earned her admiration from top **fashion editors** and **fashion photographers**. The rest is history. She became the first black model to appear on the covers of French and British *Vogue*.

C is for Naomi Campbell. Models are used to assuming various identities for clients who dictate the look. Black models are frequently expected to conform to Caucasian beauty ideals – the power of their appeal diluted and white-washed.

Campbell has not been asked to front a mainstream **make-up** campaign (unlike her supermodel sisters, and her considerably lighter-skinned and European-nosed modelling colleague Veronica Webb, who landed Revlon). Naomi therefore, although reputed to have netted around two million pounds, has never enjoyed the same financial status as her Caucasian supermodel sisters. She is often accused of behaving badly, and is reported to have issued **Karl Lagerfeld** with an ultimatum over the use of another black model in his **Chanel** show. 'It's either her or me,' she was heard to say. The racist tokenism in the fashion industry has no doubt contributed to Campbell's insecurity.

The pressure to assume a marketable identity for a whole range of clients, has inevitably led to a blonding of La Campbell, with the use of blue contact lenses, light **make-up** and straight-haired western **wigs**. Perhaps for that reason Naomi has turned to other projects for satisfaction. *Babywoman*, an album released by Epic Records with contributions from Luther Vandross and other musical luminaries, did not do well. *Swan*, a novel about the modelling world, ghost written by Caroline Upcher, fared better. Appearances in Michael Jackson's video 'Out of the Closet' and Spike Lee's film *Girl Six*, have merited positive comment, and the Fashion Café, the supermodel equivalent of the Hollywood Café for the young and photographic (a joint venture with **Christy Turlington** and Elle Macpherson), could herald a new era in designer burgers. There is always the dilemma of what to do after modelling work has dried up. In her mid-twenties, Naomi's **face** and body are most definitely her fortune, and time is on her side for the moment, but while white western beauty ideals prohibit her from displaying her real **beauty**, the potential of this woman as a role model for a generation of young women, both black and white, is severely restricted.

castings A fact of life, albeit an unpopular one, for most models. Clients, who can be anyone from **advertising** executives to **magazine** editors, photographers or **fashion designers**, may line up a casting session with a particular job in mind, or

they may agree to a **model agency**'s suggestion to see a new **face**. **Models**
may be told they are too fat, too flat-chested, too bosomy, too hippy, even too black.
Agencies will advise novices on how to handle themselves, but, say some seasoned
professionals, the amount of unnecessary personal comment on minor bodily
imperfections, or just sheer superficial judgement, never ceases to amaze.

chanel, coco One of the most influential women of the twentieth century,

Coco was born Gabrielle Bonheur Chanel in Saumur, France in 1883. Her life, in
true rags-to-riches style, was begun in a poorhouse as the illegitimate daughter
of market traders. Once famous, she denied her beginnings, and had little to do
with most of her family. Chanel had a talent for style and intense ambition to leave
behind her early poverty. She began a **millinery** business, customizing straw boaters,
and with little formal training quickly moved to **clothes**. She was fundamental in
removing the corset from the wardrobes of middle-class women, by creating loose,
soft clothing from fabrics previously used for **underwear**. In a time when lady
bicyclists in **bloomers** were arrested for indecent exposure, Chanel dared to ride a
horse in jodhpurs cut from a stable grooms' pattern. Later, she introduced costume
jewellery for all, and her perfumes utilized modern and **synthetic** smells when all
other scents still used floral notes of rose, lavender or jasmine.

She was an extremely controversial yet much loved figure. During the Second
World War Mme Chanel was amongst the first to shut down her business, a move
viewed as near-treason by the French government, who wanted their premier
haute couture house to remain open. To German soldiers she was a celebrity. Her
perfume shops enjoyed a roaring trade, as young men in fighting **uniforms** looked
for stylish souvenirs for the women back home in Germany. She in turn fraternized
with various German generals, and had a relationship with Hans Gunther von
Dincklage, sent to mobilize the French textile industry into the German war effort.
At the end of the war she was arrested and accused of collaboration; incarceration

loomed. When asked about her relationship with the German officer, she is reported to have replied, 'Really, sir, a woman of my age cannot be expected to look at his passport if she has a chance of a lover.' In a brilliant PR move she placed an announcement in the window of her shop encouraging GIs to queue for free bottles of Chanel No. 5.

Her 'less is more' approach, in combining military touches of chain and gilt with simplicity and attention to detail, was — and is — widely copied. The modern House of Chanel, run by **Karl Lagerfeld**, is easily the most prestigious of contemporary fashion houses.

children's clothes
From the earliest of times until the latter part of the eighteenth century, children's clothing replicated adult dress of the day, with all the fuss of stays, layers of petticoating and rich heavy fabrics. Up until that time, childhood itself was not really recognized — it was more a time of adult-in-training.

Then came reformers, like Jean-Jacques Rousseau, who fought for the rights of children to have a childhood space in which to grow and learn; along with this came the idea that **clothes** should accommodate their wearers for this less fettered, more carefree existence. In 1770 appears the first recorded outfit especially designed for a child. Boys wore loose ankle-length **trousers** with cotton shirts, called skeleton suits. Girls didn't enjoy the same level of comfort and convenience as their brothers and wore long cotton or muslin dresses with pantaloons. The uncovered body was still regarded as vulgar, and even young bare arms were unacceptable. Soon the skeleton suit lost popularity, and children of both sexes under five wore similar styles of cotton dresses and undergarments. Older boys were threatened with girls' clothes if they misbehaved, and some reports show how **corsetry** was effectively used to incarcerate small children when punishment was deemed necessary. Today modern childrenswear has almost returned to historical systems of dress, with miniature copies of adult designs proudly bestowed upon infants. Leather jackets, denim **jeans**, complicated **hair** and considerable jewellery are

C is for Clothes. We can make statements through our choice of clothes. Opposite right, customized condom jacket by Franco Moschino. Opposite right, men in skirts, still taboo for mainstream western men.

often found on children not yet out of their first year. Trainer **bras** and trainer **high heels** are especially popular among girls, who are given to believe that with sexual maturity comes desirability, power and status.

clothes Modern clothes have to do much more than protect the wearer from the elements. Today clothes offer complicated and detailed information about identity. One person may have several identities, so that '**uniforms**' for school or office may differ considerably from clothes chosen for leisure time. But it's not just the garments themselves that we display proudly, or ask others to take an interest in. Branding, a relatively modern trend, is the manifestation of consumerism at its most competitive. **Sportswear** companies, for example, encourage ideas of conquest in their logos (Nike means victor) and **streetstyles** also insist on membership through clothing association. The fashion industry offers yet another chance to belong to a community of like-minded dressers. In the mid-eighties came an epidemic of expensively priced clothes, complete with the designer's signature or logo prominently displayed on the

C is for Clothes: Designers may have something to say about gender. Right, Alexander McQueen presents an anti-glamour statement for women, while Dolce & Gabbana feminize their menswear.

outside of the garment, quickly followed by the designer **t-shirt**, as **fashion designers** realized that their names were just as marketable as their clothing designs.

codpiece

One of the few items of masculine clothing (worn in the 1500s) that openly sexualized the body. Worn like a stiff or built-up pouch over the penis, this item of attire would be immaculately embroidered and bejewelled. King Henry VIII favoured a codpiece of magnificent proportions over his tights; he appeared resplendent in gold jewellery and pioneered the look of medallion man as far back as the sixteenth century.

corsetry

In recent seasons corsets have been offered by a variety of designers, including **Gianni Versace**, as showy under-the-suit staple. Since **Vivienne Westwood** first designed the 'stature of liberty' corset in the mid-eighties to accessorize her mini crini, and **Jean-Paul Gaultier** began experimenting with

stylistic ideas of lacing and bodily confinement, a whole generation of women have sampled the hourglass effect of such satiny restriction. The practice of waist reduction has existed in England for hundreds of years, and the focus on small waists resurfaces whenever **fashion designers** want to sell ideas of petiteness and grace. Belts, waistbands, seams and of course corsets are all popular design statements. Even hipsters, which offer a bare-waisted view, rely on a svelte and streamlined waist for maximum effect.

cowboys

Every business has them, and fashion is no exception. They prey on young women hoping to become **models**. They are usually photographers who say they have contacts with **model agencies**, and set up photo shoots promising entry to the business. Some charge hundreds of pounds for an amateur set of prints and have no intentions beyond ripping off young hopefuls. Do not hand over any money to these scumbags. Do report them to the Association of Modelling Agencies (AMA).

crawford, cindy

Born in 1966, her full name is Cynthia Anne Crawford. Reputedly amongst the most professional and intelligent of the early **supermodel** batch, Ms Crawford was the first to recognize her commercial potential, and has since marketed herself with ruthless business flair. Through a best-selling **swimsuit** calendar, a fitness videos, her own cable channel show *House of Style* and a lucrative contract with soft drinks giants Pepsi, she has broken down traditional barriers that previously restricted model practices. She sees herself as the president who owns the product.

The second of three daughters from a blue-collar family, her first big break came when her photograph as co-ed of the week attracted Clairol representatives. After employing her for a hairstyling demonstration in Chicago, she was put onto the local **model agency**. But her refusal to remove her now-famous mole caused aggravation, and early test pictures hid the offending blemish in shadow. After graduating she went to Europe to gather all-important magazine editorial. She didn't stay long; her luscious locks were cut, much to her distress, and at eighteen she was asked to model nude. When she later found herself lying in the surf with a face-pack on for over two hours, waves submerging her head, she thought of calling it a day. But she didn't. She succeeded in marketing her mole to her advantage, and now promotes Revlon and a host of other cosmetics. She met film actor Richard Gere in 1988 and turned her attention to a film career. She refused some work because of sex scenes and allegedly laughed so hard during a reading for a poorly-scripted blockbuster, that onlookers were forced to assume lack of commitment. Now separated from Gere after a brief marriage, she continues to exhibit a maverick streak, but her earnings – around the three million dollar mark – show no sign of decreasing. With her cheesecake looks and wholesome Ms Universe mass-market appeal, some don't think she merits the attention she gets. But her ability should not be judged on the runway alone. Her unquestionable superiority lies in providing a bridge from the previously aloof world of catwalk **modelling**, straight to the heart of the commercially insatiable middle-American consumer. She has paved the way for her supersisters, who now use her marketing techniques to broaden their own financial empires. I hope they've all written her perfumed thank you notes.

cycles The fashion industry is endlessly cyclical, repeatedly working and re-working old ideas into new. Many have noted that if they stand still long enough, refusing to change fashions in accordance with progressing styles, their **clothes** will be subject to gentle teasing, perhaps ridicule, but eventually they will acquire a hip status and mainstream popularity once more. In climates of confident expansion and discovery, such as the sixties, women's **clothes** exhibited a child-like, wide-eyed awe at new technologies and inventions. Nostalgia is frequently employed to evoke security and familiarity in times of upheaval. Fashion can even reflect stock market tendencies; skirt lengths fell from above-knee flapper styles to mid-calf on the eve of the 1929 stock market crash and in Britain journalists have pointed to the crash of 1987, when the Thatcherite bubble burst and with it the balloon-like skirt shape engineered by **Christian Lacroix**.

dior, christian

The name Dior is thoroughly associated with the **New Look**. During his short life, Christian Dior created an *haute couture* and ready to wear or *prêt à porter* business that has survived headed by Italian **fashion designer** Gianfranco Ferre. Born in France in 1905, Dior was the son of an affluent fertilizer manufacturer. He wanted to study architecture, but was pressurized into politics by his family. He abandoned his studies, however, and opened a small art gallery with a friend. During the depression, when his father's business was wiped out, he sought refuge in Russia, but became disillusioned with Soviet communism. After returning to **Paris**, he lived hand-to-mouth for many years, at one point becoming so ill he was sent to Spain for a rest-cure. On his return to Paris he began to draw and sold

D is for Dior. The nostalgic silhouette of the New Look reappears 40 years on, reproduced by Christian Dior.

sketches to newspapers. He eventually joined the house of Lelong, learning many skills, especially the art of well-made **clothes**. In 1946 he set up his own business and in the brief time until his death in 1957 made a huge impact with his collections, adored by **fashion editors** everywhere.

dolce & gabbana An Italian design duo. Stefano Gabbana is the younger of the two. Both are in their thirties and after ten years in the business (they produce **menswear** ranges as well as perfume and the younger line D&G) have established a reputation for setting trends and creating dramatic photo opportunities with their provocative (flirt factor 10) clothes. Their first collection entitled 'real woman' paved the way for a preoccupation with bosoms and **bottoms** while celebrating home-grown sex goddesses like Sophia Loren and Anna Magnani. In **interviews** they say they have moved on or grown up, and in a continual exploration of Italian femininity they currently rework the Sicilian widow, for a catwalk appearance of catholic splendour. Meanwhile black, their favoured colour, is inspired by Italian grandmothers and the volcanic island of Stromboli. They are usually the first show in the **Milan** calendar and enjoy considerable press attention. The entrance to their showroom during this time is crammed with paparazzi waiting for **supermodels** or Isabella Rossellini, their signature mannequin, to arrive.

dress reform In the middle of the nineteenth century, American and European activists campaigning for women's rights, flouted strict feminine dress codes of the day by introducing 'reform fashions'. **Amelia Bloomer** and members of

D is for Dress Reform: Throughout the years women have fought for the right to wear masculine clothes. Vivienne Westwood emphasizes her trouser suit design with traditional touches.

the 'anti-crinoline' movement objected to the **clothes** of the day, which required not only layers of heavy fabric and ornamentation, but restrictive **corsetry** that resulted in physical damage. The Bloomer (which was considered to be a modified **trouser** and therefore the territory of men) was worn in public as an act of defiance by those brave enough to bear the verbal abuse, and even physical attack, that resulted. Later, the split skirt, simpler styles and softer fabrics became acceptable. **Coco Chanel** did much to further practicality and comfort, and is generally credited as the inventor of twentieth century woman's fashion. Her first successful designs, which displayed a preference for simple lines and plain cloth, were known as the 'poor look'.

environmental awareness Until recently there's been very little to choose from if you want to look both good and 'green'; but as more manufacturers wake up to the fact that **clothes** cannot continue to cost the earth, solutions are beginning to come. They range from eco-conscious manufacturing processes and fabrics, to **recycling** and eco-rating schemes.

Currently, many **synthetic** fabrics are derived from finite fuel resources such as crude oil, natural gas and other petrochemicals. Large amounts of energy and water go into the processes of cooling and removal of hazardous waste. Some

E is for Environmental Awareness. The use of fabrics that do not damage the environment in their production is fashionable from time to time. But rubber, plastic and other chemically made fabrics are currently enjoying popularity.

believe that a staggering 50 per cent or more of the UK's nitrous oxide emissions are a result of Nylon manufacturing alone. The dying of fabrics, when synthetic petrochemical components are used in conjunction with toxic metal fixers, can be the most polluting stage of production, resulting in vast quantities of toxic substances being released into the environment. Even the finish applied to many crease-resistant clothes is only made possible with the use of formaldehyde resin, an extremely potent chemical which can cause asthma, dizziness, headaches and skin complaints. And when we've finished with our clothes, then what? Of the waste deposited in landfill sites, dumped at sea, or incinerated to release more foul gases, textiles make up a hefty 2.1 per cent.

Cotton is possibly the most obvious fabric to choose if you want to dress green. Given that around 50 per cent of our garments contain some cotton, the need for cotton that is organically produced, unbleached, undyed and untreated, thus making it truly biodegradable, is urgent. The prohibitive factor for both producers and consumers is cost. Without the aid of growth enhancers and pest controls, yield can drop by 40 per cent. However, more and more people are willing to pay more for organic cloth – sufferers of skin complaints and allergies (now on the increase) most particularly so. Companies who can provide chemical-free clothing made from organically grown cotton are on the increase.

There is growing interest in other natural fibres. Hemp, made from the cannabis plant, was grown throughout Europe until last century. It grows quickly and easily and was a traditional fabric used to make a variety of clothes as well as canvas, rope, sackcloth and paper. Use gradually declined as cotton, generally thought to be more versatile, became available through import. The little hemp still grown was further hit when it was outlawed in 1971, following concerns surrounding marijuana cultivation. Drug hysteria under control, hemp is now grown in low-narcotic varieties, and is being used to manufacture clothes again.

But it's very small-scale — there are only two thousand acres currently being grown in the UK.

Tencel is made with the wood pulp of specially harvested trees. It uses a manufacturing process that recycles nearly all of the organic solvents, so that 99 per cent of the effluent is water. Tencel has been hailed as the textile miracle of the decade. It is durable and soft, with fibres that shrink far less than other natural thread, and has the ability to 'take on the personality' of almost any fabric. Highstreet designers like Next have used it to make a denim look-alike fabric, and **Katharine Hamnett**, a strong advocate of green issues, has frequently included it amongst her designs.

Another advance is the Eco-Check Index, which will give clothing companies a rating based on their environmental performance. This will certainly be a step forward, but while ratings in areas like energy consumption are relatively easy to establish, the cost of human **labour** may be harder to quantify.

But these new fibres, greener production methods and eco-labels are still only a drop in the ocean. Fashion is by its very nature a wasteful industry, and more thought about the whole ethos of fashion consumption is vital. The brightest greens in the fashion world in my view are the many smaller designers who have already begun a recycling culture; so far it has gained them little recognition. They are in fact the true innovators in the fashion world, and they leave the extravagant and excessively indulgent catwalk kings and queens way behind.

eating disorders When the fashion industry celebrates the **waif**, it exempts itself from taking responsibility about the messages it offers to young women about their bodies. We are now more conscious than ever that many women achieve their skeletal looks through eating disorders, which kill. Anorexia — the

refusal to eat, or obsessional control of food intake – affects up to forty thousand girls of secondary school age in the UK. Bulimia – a binge and purge method of controlling weight by vomiting or laxative abuse – affects some one hundred thousand women. Some reports suggest that 50 per cent of **British** women struggle with some kind of disordered eating pattern.

In Fashionland, whatever else is '**out**' as spring gives way to autumn and autumn turns into spring, thin is always 'in'. How many fashion **magazines** carry diet and 'lose weight fast' features in between their 'new look' fashion pages? This new look is nothing new at all, just another chapter in a long-running cultural scheme that has the majority of women at war with their bodies. If the fashion industry creates a **fantasy** of false femininity, then the diet industry pedals a poisonous lie. Relentless brainwashing on the theme of 'thinness equals happiness and desirability' is all-embracing, and a multi-million pound diet food industry is validated in the process.

It is well-nigh impossible not to absorb this message – our bodies aren't good enough. Girls learn to restrict their consumption from observing their mothers and older sisters – perpetually dissatisfied with their healthy bodies – struggling with diets. We even have a language that reminds us of the penalty for living in bodies larger than the approved size. Words like '**outsize**' and 'overweight' immediately communicate disapproval. The cultural message to women is unmistakable – take up less space. This, in a world where women are still fighting to claim a foothold, serves as a powerful emotional and physical restraint. If a woman is preoccupied with herself and the inadequacy of her body to the point of life and death, she will not contribute to the world outside with her presence, her energy and her voice. Naomi Wolf, and others, target dieting as the most potent political sedative in women's history.

The bravery of the women who fight these disorders – for that's what they are doing every day – is immense. They fight to understand the destructive force within.

For the fashion industry, thinness amongst models is a prized state. Some of the top earners look as though they also have eating disorders. Ordinary adolescent women are perplexed. How can it be wrong to starve themselves, when lavishly paid fashion industry role models look like they do the same?

Anorexics and bulimics may progress through a whole range of 'disciplines'; survivors often adopt punishing exercise routines to keep their bodies in check. Others resort to a catalogue of mutilation, including jaw-wiring, stomach-stapling, liposuction and plastic surgery. They are not victims, they are just fighting the wrong enemy, using their energy and creativity to wage war on themselves instead of doing battle with a culture that systematically undervalues the majority of women.

evangelista, linda

Brought up in Toronto of Italian parentage, Linda Evangelista is the prima diva of the **modelling** world. Her career began early (she was modelling bridesmaids' dresses at six) and due to her acute business sense and ability to reinvent herself, she continues to be amongst the most in demand of all. At sixteen she entered the local Miss Teen Niagra **beauty** contest and was spotted by a **New York** scout. At eighteen she was doing **Calvin Klein** commercials. She had long dark **hair**, but in what became the career move of the century, she cut it off and dyed it **blonde**. She says she was in tears, holding photographer Peter Lindenbergh's hand, as her locks fell to the floor. She has of course enjoyed **supermodel** status ever since.

More popular with women than men, Ms Evangelista has worked at her trade. She understands the gift she has been given. She told Michael Gross in *Model* 'Every day I thank God for my looks because I know where I'd be without them.' She works to improve on what she has for the camera, for example using a tip given to her by **fashion photographer** Stephen Meisel of opening her mouth in pictures to prevent her chin from looking weak. She takes a very intense and professional interest in her work, using her appearance and the transformation she can effect with **make-up** and hairstyle, together with her body, to conjure a look. Top **fashion photographers** say she does not act for the camera, but offers a more refined craft, evoking the spirit of the person she is playing. When shoots aren't going well, she makes her dissatisfaction known, earning her the title of 'Evilangelista', but justifies her pique as that of a professional trying to get the job done in the best way.

She is at the top of her profession, and like everyone in pole position has to deal with jealousy. When Linda Evangelista's phone rang at three in the morning just before the **Paris *haute couture*** shows, she was told her friend **Karl Lagerfeld** needed her urgently for a fitting. She rushed over to oblige, but found the studio shut. Rumours were rife as to who it could have been; Ms Evangelista no doubt needed a touch extra concealer under her eyes the following morning. She has rejected lucrative but sometimes prohibitive cosmetics contracts, preferring to work where, and with whom, she wants; she is not attracted to Hollywood or acting. In her early thirties, Ms Evangelista's presence on the international catwalk is a triumph in an industry that retires its female players early. Her ability to ignore the built-in sell-by date and her refusal to promote one corporate vision of femininity are important parts of her appeal.

fab The fashion world's most over-used adjective. I've said it from time to time, but I'm trying to give it up.

face Linda Evangelista claims to have a frowny mouth and a crooked face. 'I'd like to have a happy mouth. People ask if I've had a nose job. If I had, would I have chosen a nose like this?' Ms Evangelista, like so many of us, is preoccupied with the facial furniture she owns. Perhaps the fact that she must see so many mirror images of herself (albeit front covers) staring from street corners, hated conk planted centre stage, causes irritation. No one else has noticed, Linda, you are much more to us than your nose.

F is for Fantasy. Catwalk shows are a time for male designers to indulge their desire for the fantasy woman. Nobody does it with more conviction than French designer Thierry Mugler.

In early times, facial protrusions and other lumps and bumps were examined in detail. In the days of Classical Rome, face-reading was an established profession, and face and character were intricately related. Wax faces of dead ancestors were cast and proudly displayed on the sideboard for visiting guests to enjoy. In western Europe physiognomy (the art of judging character from facial features) was first posited by astrologer Michael Scot in 1272. Later Johann Kaspar Lavater, the son of a physician in Zurich, rose to fame with his *Essays in Physiognomy* which appeared in the 1770s. His work was translated into many languages, and monarchs, emperors and leaders from all over the world sought his opinions, which were delivered with considerable aplomb. Unsurprisingly there were choice observations on women:

> A woman with a deeply concave root of the nose, a full bosom, and a somewhat projecting canine tooth, will…lead away the whole herd of grovelling [male] voluptuaries. The worst prostitutes brought before the spiritual courts are always of this conformation. Avoid it as a pestilence.

Witch-hunters, of course made ample use of this pseudo-science, and disposed of those that were 'blear-eyed, pale, foul and full of wrinkles'. Popular language still offers remnants of our desire to deduce personality or character from the arrangement of features we see. But appearances are, of course deceptive. Bare-faced lies can be told by those careful enough to control their facial composure while delivering a whopper.

fairy-tales
The fashion world is happy to market itself as one big fairy-tale world with a happy ending. Beautiful maidens – **supermodels** of course; Prince Charming types – dashing **fashion photographers**. The Fairy Godmother? An indulgent and generous **fashion designer**, who waves a magic wand and kits out said beauty in full sartorial splendour. Wicked **witches**? Well, there's always some

severe-faced **fashion editor** threatening to kill off the beautiful lead who's not **face** of the moment anymore, or take away the fairy godmother's power because nobody is wearing fuchsia and lime this year anyway. Fairy-tales are ancient stories which often praise demure, passive women and condemn powerful ones. We understand that Cinderella's beauty and her fine dress are the reasons she is able to capture the prince. To remind him of her exquisite femininity she leaves a shoe, not just any old shoe, but a tiny glass court shoe with a heel. Snow White, our dopey but beautiful heroine, flees her home to escape the wrath of the wicked Queen, who's got it in for her because she's young and pretty and the Queen is getting on a bit. Told to wide-eyed girls of three or four, these tales are powerful preparation for a lifetime of uneasiness around appearance. Today we invest the fashion and **beauty** industries with magical powers to ensure our happiness, while the **advertising** community uses modernday spells and technological trickery to bewitch us into a consumer trance. In a competitive world where beauty is marketed as a prerequisite to love and success, women are frequently encouraged to consult the mirror, mirror on the wall, for proof of who is the fairest of them all.

fake Advertising campaigns make pretty pictures – and that's it. Once this fakery is taken for granted you can observe the imagery you are offered with some objectivity, and have fun with fashion, **clothes** and **make-up**.

fantasy As we've seen, the fashion industry sells fantasy in many forms. Dream-like clothes creating illusions of mythical femininity are staple fare among catwalk collections. For some designers, like Thierry Mugler, however, fantasy is the main course. His **shows** have combined exaggerated stage costume with exotic sexual **uniform** for an image of woman as mattress, or supervixen. It has been observed that male **fashion designers** may not always be designing for the woman they see before them, but for the woman they would actually like to be.

fashion buyers

Fashion buyers are a cross between fashion visionary and city broker. They are responsible for stocking their shops with a wide range of desirable **clothes**. It is their job to satisfy customer demand while making a profit for their employer. It's a pressure job. Buyers must be thoroughly in-the-know as far as trends are concerned; they may employ the services of **prediction agencies** or a consultancy bureaux, as well as visiting exhibitions and **shows** like the giant fabric fairs. They will make choices about the clothes they buy based on company purchasing strategy; this will be determined by customer profile (their age and socio-economic status); the number of lines the shop wants to offer; assortment; quality; and degree of exclusivity. Large stores can insist on exclusivity and enter into agreements that prohibit **fashion designers** selling to other shops in the street or town. This can be especially difficult for young designers starting out, who may only be selling small amounts to a powerful store. Equally a buyer can support the growth of new designers, especially if backed by a chain of stores. Buyers cannot afford to make mistakes, and must not be influenced by sensationalized fashion reporting. It is they who decide what a designer will actually manufacture. One or two of the more sensational outfits might be purchased, but purely for front-of-house display. If a line does not sell, profit is lost as clothes are knocked down at sale time to clear the shop floor for the next season's deliveries. The more faddish the garment, the greater the risk. Sale time is an opportunity to write off buying mistakes, but a buyer who relies on this method of clearance will swiftly be out of a job.

fashion designers

Every industry has its darlings, and designers are ours. Temperamental, petulant, eccentric, permanently in the land of 'My Little Pony' – this is how outsiders imagine the world of the fashion designer. In reality these people have to be skilled business women and men, able to survive in a competitive field. Many designers lament the lack of time for the creative process, as other priorities impinge – the management of staff, post-production on collections, manufacturing, selling, licensing. In fact the ready-to-wear, or *prêt à porter* collections you and I see on a twice-yearly basis are but a small part of the working year. They are given by far the most media attention, and the **shows** act for a designer in much the same way as **advertising**, consolidating brand image in our minds. Aspirational imagery of superbeauties in **fantasy** clothes influences our choices at the cosmetics or perfumes counter. Top houses do not necessarily expect to sell their **clothes** at a big show, but recognize the need to exhibit in order to sustain sales of associated products.

fashion editors An exotic variety of journalists, whose dedication to the job of spotting and writing about talent knows no bounds. They are frequently frustrated when the news desk doesn't take them seriously, and their carefully worded prose is dropped at the last minute for a frontline report of what royalty is wearing. But they are queens in their own domain; at show time fashion editors are the front-row guests of every fashion **public relations** officer.

There is much trivia written about fashion editors, mostly by those on the outside; after all, they are a mysterious and powerful group of people. Here, for those of you who suspected that all you have to do is swing a **Prada** handbag about the place and make like Patsy in *Ab-Fab*, is the lowdown. Yes, fashion editors do wear dark glasses a lot; they reason that sitting in the front row of any catwalk **show** is stressful on the retina when the lights are turned to flood; others value the disguise when it comes to nodding off or glazing over, a common symptom of show fatigue. If a hack should turn in a less than flattering review of a show they might find their seating arrangements slightly rearranged next time round. Some designers even award seats in direct relation to how much press they received last season. Fashion editors 'between jobs' have found themselves shunted to the back; in this industry at least, it's not who you know, but who you write for. At *The Clothes Show* we are usually positioned three rows back, which sadly means we don't have to wear dark glasses – but we all like to anyway! Some fashion editors make notes and drawings of each show. These will later be used to call in **clothes** for individual **fashion shoots**. The **fantasy** that fashion editors wear the particular designer labels to each individual show still exists; but with up to ten shows a day there isn't time, so most throw on something black first thing in the morning and leave it there all day. Travel takes up a large part of the calendar, and many fashion hacks carry a portable PC to ensure deadline delivery. During show time **fashion designers** must be wined and dined to procure **advertising**, and interest must be displayed – or feigned – at all times. But the backscratching is mutual; a powerful journalist can do much to support or damage the profile of any design house or designer, so presents and lavish attention are bestowed on those with mighty pens.

fashion photographers

Fashion photography is a high-profile profession that has until recently been almost exclusively about men photographing women. Recent times have seen some women photographers make considerable, sometimes controversial, impact. Corrine Day began by photographing her friend **Kate Moss**; she gets her inspiration from her own life and contemporaries, forging an anti-fashion style that does not rely on elaborate **make-up** and **hair** statements. Ellen von Unwerth, an ex-model, is best known for her black and white imagery which evokes filmic atmospheres, where models may be moving in and out of frame. Ellen's women are dramatic, glamorous and self-motivated, rarely captured offering the standard flirting and pouting postures that so many male photographers favour. Now that the market is beginning to open up, female image-makers are getting access to **advertising** campaigns and prestigious editorial. As a result, some welcome diversity is creeping into the images of femininity we consumers are presented with.

Fashion photography is generally considered to have started in 1913, when De Meyer (a baron by marriage) began work for the publisher Condé Nast who had recently purchased American *Vogue*. He became known for his pictures of society women in their gowns, making much more of the photograph than traditional portraiture of the time. Experimenting with backlighting and the sparkle of beads, sequins and other shiny elements on the clothes, he is acknowledged as the pioneer of a craft that is fundamental to the way we now communicate ideas of **beauty** and femininity. Fashion photography grew in popularity and in the thirties **London**-born Cecil Beaton became one of the best known photographers in the world, using artificial backdrops and mirrors to create a composition for his subjects. Norman Parkinson, who specialized in portraits of débutantes, after working as a military photographer during the war, achieved great success in the fashion world and royal circles. Society women were the mannequins of the day, poses were static and regal. Richard Avedon changed things considerably when, in 1944, he persuaded the **New York** branch of the department store Bonwit Teller to lend him some high fashion **clothes** for a shoot. **Models** began to wear designer clothes for fashion stories, but still looked and acted like society women. Avedon used unfamiliar settings like zoos and NASA launch pads, instructing his models to move around without paying attention to the camera, beginning a trend that continues to influence today's lensmen and women. In the sixties, the appeal of untitled and ordinary young women like Jean Shrimpton, Penelope Tree and Twiggy was captured by **British** photographers. In a time of freedom and experimentation, where sex was no longer taboo, a new element to the image began to materialize, and models, proud of their emerging sexuality, partied in front of the camera. David Bailey and Terence Donovan were there to join in, and are still very much in demand today. In the last thirty years, fashion photography has become a highly desirable career option, producing a multitude of happy snappers who repackage ordinary femininity into a vision of heavenly perfection. Some, like New Yorker Stephen Meisel, have taken on a Svengali-like persona, and are much in demand from advertising agencies.

There are unsung others, however, who are invaluable to the world of fashion photography. They are the foot soldiers at the front-line, who battle to set up a tripod on a platform packed with hundreds of other bodies, or who squeeze themselves into the moats around large runways. **Show** photography is poles apart from the airy studio world of editorial and advertising photography. British photographer Charlotte Macpherson is one of the few women players who have chosen to operate in this macho and highly competitive environment. Every few months she sets off round the fashion world (**Milan**, London, **Paris** and New York) for a month-long gruelling assignment. Her hours will be long and her day spent in cramped, uncomfortable, sometimes dangerous positions. With up to ten shows per day, and ten to thirty rolls of film designated to each show, the pressure to document catwalk and backstage goings-on is enormous. These people, along with film crews, bring us the first pictures of the newest collections. **Fashion editors** and their show photographers enjoy a relationship of mutual respect as both work late into the night selecting imagery for the following morning's stories back in Britain.

fashion shoots Fashion editors will plan their shoots months in

advance, carefully choosing a team of experts. In some cases celebrity **fashion photographers** dictate the team, the location and the terms, and will liaise with the art director on concept. Space within a top magazine is very pressured. **Big** names will barter for the maximum pages; the bigger the reputation, the bigger the shoot and budget. Some big names edit their own contact photographs, refusing to allow photos to be reproduced unless full page. On less precious publications, a fashion editor and her assistant will conduct the operation, frequently featuring only the clothes of valued advertisers. In any shoot a variety of devices are employed to make the **clothes** and the woman look fantastic. Apart from the services of **hair** and **make-up** specialists, the **stylist** will fit the clothes around the body of the model to achieve the best effect. This means using bulldog clips, pins and tapes to hold it all together. **Models** may have tape underneath their **breasts** to enhance cleavage, **hair**pieces for fullness, and their **feet** crammed into shoes that are too small. While they hold a fixed smile to camera, lighting and light deflector are carefully placed to bleach out any wrinkles. Then eyes and teeth will be whitened on the finished print. Bear this in mind when you next compare yourself to these beauties – and give yourself a break.

fashion victims
When being in fashion is so important that suitability, function and comfort of clothing are of no importance at all, then a fashion victim is born. Those of us that have staggered across uneven roads and pavements in nine-inch **platforms** like drunken totties know how it feels. In the mid-eighties, bald and bedecked in bondage strides, I frequently had to decline offers of help from old ladies; when my ripped jeans were so ripped that entry was barred from even the most insalubrious drinking establishments (and my companion was cautioned by a policeman for indecent exposure), 'fashion victim' was certainly a term bandied about in my direction. But I took little notice. My school report from Feltham Comprehensive read: 'Caryn will not get a good job by being the most fashionable person in the school.' I was out to prove them wrong.

feet
Naomi Campbell dislikes her feet, partly because she says they have hard skin from ballet, but mostly we suspect because they are a perfectly healthy size nine. Mmm, it's that size thing again. The refusal on the part of the **British** Shoe Corporation to provide British women with **footwear** to fit is the problem here. Shoe sizes do not keep pace with our own growth, and while the popular display size to be found in windows remains a miniature four, consumers needing sizes over six will be hard pressed to enjoy the same variety given to the tiny-toed punters among us.

feminism
A few designers, such as Karen Savage, have explored the fertile terrain of feminism in their work. Savage's 'Babe' and 'Bitch' **T-shirts** are to be seen on chests up and down the country. (Babe, on the front, is what the wearer might be called as she approaches a building site, and Bitch on the reverse we've

all heard as we pass without having delivered a smile.) Early feminists challenged dress codes of the day in order to bring to attention their dissatisfaction with restrictive roles and opportunities for women. More recently came the alleged burning of the **bra** in the seventies; this has since been dismissed by some female scholars as a smokescreen employed by the media to ridicule serious issues. But it does represent the desire many women had to rid themselves of the trappings of femininity, just like their earlier sisters. Dungarees, formerly made of a fabric called dungaree from the Hindi word *dungri* (a coarse Indian calico), became the **uniform**

F is for Fake; The hair, the make-up and the clothes all play a part in the fashion industry's skill at faking it. Backstage at Paco Rabanne a model waits to be someone else.

of the movement, as women both sides of the Atlantic attempted to take as little interest in their appearance as possible.

Contemporary feminists tend to agree that all accoutrements of femininity, **lipstick**, **high heels** and the lot — can be supportive allies in the battle for equality; women can enjoy **make-up** and fashion because they want to, not because they feel they have to. But this is complicated territory in times when fashion can still reduce women to cleavages and thighs; witness celebrated writer Germaine Greer attacking Suzanne Moore because she didn't look like a feminist, wore too much lipstick, sported high heels and overdid the hairspray.

fetish Coined by Portuguese sailors hundreds of years ago, 'fetish' described the fertility effigies African tribes worshipped. Later Freud took up the term and said that when it comes to **clothes**, every woman is a fetishist. Fetish clothes are frequently used to suggest power through sexual domination. A sortie through any

'**fantasy**' catalogue will reveal an assortment of styles and designs that exaggerate or caricature sexual features. For women **breasts**, thighs, **bottoms** and **feet** are given utmost attention, and functionalism is about ease of sexual activity. Sometimes fabrics themselves are invested with potency; leather, rubber and plastic are popularly employed to suggest skin that can be marked or torn but will not yield to pain. Fetish clothing, especially rubberwear, requires considerable maintenance; talcum powder helps in getting the stuff on, and once removed it must be stored in dark closets, where the light cannot disintegrate it. In recent seasons fetishwear has found its way onto the catwalk, with vinyl, PVC and lycra featuring among the most unlikely designer offerings. Shock thresholds have dissolved as mainstream and clubland designers have blurred the boundaries between fashion and fetishwear.

flat shoes
There is always the assumption that flat shoes are not sexy. Whether it be kickers, court shoe pumps, trainers or deck shoes, we understand that practicality precludes sexiness; comfort for women is frumpy, discomfort is

attractive. In the eighties, Dr Marten's enjoyed huge popularity amongst a new generation of women searching for practical **footwear** in the pre-trainer era. Suddenly clubland was awash with booted beauties fusing femininity with militancy, having the time of their lives dancing the night away and then legging it for the night bus. At last sensible shoes were high fashion, and fashion designers took note. **Jean-Paul Gaultier** accessorized his womenswear with polished silver toe-capped versions, while John Richmond and his partner Maria Cornejo teamed their **clothes** with DMs and shoe jewellery. Meanwhile the house of Red or Dead, begun by Wayne Hemmingway, reinvented the DM with **wet look**, tartan and velvet designs.

footbinding
From AD 1100 in China and parts of Korea footbinding was correct procedure for the upper classes. Women were instructed to restrict the growth of their daughters' **feet** by breaking the bones over and over again, and binding them tightly into foul-smelling, rotting stumps which were then covered by exquisitely embroidered shoes, little more than three inches in length. There were obsessive rules for the manufacture and care of these tiny feet – known as lotus hooks – which involved set procedures on size of bandage, intervals between bandaging, length of the 'correct foot'. There were even directions for sitting and standing once feet were bound, as well as rituals concerning the washing of the gangrenous reshaped feet. Once a small girl had been crippled (binding began for some at two years old) all movement was terminated. Women could only hobble slowly in extreme pain or be carried. Social justification was eligibility for marriage, but privately Chinese men were aroused by helpless women with small dainty feet in much the same way that many western men are attracted to distorted arches in **high heels**. Historical accounts have survived to show that men enjoyed squeezing the stumps to cause pain, smelling them, and stuffing them into their mouths, as well as drinking a variety of fluids from the miniature shoes. But footbinding is not the alien concept we westerners like to think it is. Louis XV's

mistress, Madame Pompadour, accentuated her tiny feet by wearing high heels that curved into a small base. The heel became known as the Pompadour heel and for a while women of the French court mutilated their own feet and hobbled in pain like their Chinese sisters. As recently as the 1950s, women squeezed themselves into smaller sizes than they actually were, and some even amputated toes to fit the narrow styles. Traditional styles for women today still attempt to reduce the size of the foot with a heel, as well as tapering toes into cramped spaces.

footwear
Like all accessories, shoes keep in line with the latest fashions. **Gucci** produce their own high-fashion item for feet every season, and **Miuccia Prada** currently dominates the catwalk scene with her own vision of fashionable footwear. There are also specialist shoe designers and in Britain a plethora of new young shoe designers, like John Moore, Elizabeth Stuart Smith, Emma Hope and Christine Ahrens, emerged to inject the mainstream footwear industry with some much-needed inspiration. Two of this group, Patrick Cox and Jimmy Choo, now have footwear empires of their own, and all have done much to inspire a whole new generation of novices to take up shoe design. New talent continues to spill out of our colleges, especially Cordwainers College, founded in 1887.

Shoemaking was originally a masculine trade. In medieval **London**, shoemakers worked in areas around the Royal Exchange. They formed a guild to ensure quality of work and materials, the Guild of Cordwainers was one of the earliest. This name was taken from Cordova, a town in Spain providing the best leather. Just like **clothes** of the day, shoes were made to order and to the specific size of the client. In 1792 John Smith of Norwich abandoned the practice of measuring and produced a set of ready-made boots to be tried on and purchased on the spot. Production then geared up to cater for a wider audience. In 1794, the first retail boot store surfaced in America. Shoe sizing became standardized, using the traditional measuring system of a zero point at four inches, and an advance of two thirds of an inch to size thirteen for children. For adults size one began at eight and two thirds inches, and still does to this day in Britain.

Up until the mid-1800s shoemakers were tradespeople, but with the advent of the fashion house, the idea of a designed shoe emerged. A Parisian, Pinnet, opened an elegant establishment in 1863, catering to the rich visitors of couturiers. The Pinnet heel retained its popularity into the 1930s. By now men's shoes had become dull brogues with none of the flamboyance of earlier periods. Male shoe designers concentrated on women's shoes to make their artistic mark. **High heels** accompanied the **New Look** in the forties and women shortened their steps in shoes that prohibited running, striding or any kind of marching. Italian designer Salvatore Ferragamo, who had responded to wartime leather shortages with substitute materials like fish skins, Cellophane, canvas and cork, surfaced as an international force. Later the Parisian Vivier, who worked with **Christian Dior**, became the first shoemaker to share an equal billing with a couturier on the mass-produced collection which complemented Dior's designs. One of the greatest contemporary shoe designers is Manolo Blahnik. Born in the Canary Isles, he trained as a theatre

designer, but was encouraged by the legendary Diana Vreeland to design shoes. He moved to London and set up his shop in 1973; he has since designed for many of the international fashion élite, including **Calvin Klein**, **Yves Saint Laurent**, **Zandra Rhodes** and **Rifat Ozbek**, besides producing his own collections four times a year.

fragrance industry One of the most lucrative aspects of any

couture house, the fragrance division can outsell all other divisions combined. These luxury products with designer labels don't require the wearers to be thin, young, rich or even fashion-conscious, so their appeal is vast. Anyone can join the club. **Coco Chanel** was one of the first to recognize the consumer's need to belong as well as importance of diversification for the future of her own business. She launched Chanel No. 5 in 1921, which still achieves sales of hundreds of millions of pounds as a number one seller. Other design houses followed. Jean Patou lauched Joy in 1933, and Nina Ricci followed in 1948 with L'Air du Temps. These three still rank among the world's topselling smells. Coco Chanel sold her perfume to a private American cosmetics manufacturer, a move she later bitterly regretted when the fragrance industry expanded. In fact many designers and design houses

F is for Fur. Anti-fur debates can be subtly highlighted by the designers themselves. Here Franco Moschino sticks two fingers up to the real thing, while celebrating a novel alternative.

don't harvest the entire profit from their successful scents, as giant conglomerates often own the licence. France's L'Oreal owns **Ralph Lauren** perfumes, and Japan's Shiseido owns both **Jean-Paul Gaultier** and **Issey Miyake** perfumes.

Large companies spend huge amounts on **advertising** budgets to announce the arrival of a product, and with over two hundred fragrance launches during one

Christmas period alone, competition is unbelievably stiff. **Christian Lacroix**'s C'est La Vie, launched by the French luxury holding Moet Hennessy Louis Vitton in the early nineties, never found its audience, despite an alleged $40 million advertising budget. But consumers will pay top money, as the success of Joy – advertised as the world's most expensive perfume with ten thousand six hundred jasmine flowers and forty eight dozen roses needed to create each ounce – will testify. Those who have cracked the market have embraced the idea of lifestyle fragrances, plugging into the pretend world of a fictitious character. Charlie, launched in the seventies, was the first perfume to do this successfully, and featured a succession of swingy-haired blondes. It has since been re-marketed, with Claudia Schiffer as the latest 'Charlie-girl'.

fur

In an anti-fur ad from People for the Ethical Treatment of Animals, German **supermodel** Nadja Auermann poses naked with the slogan 'I'd rather go naked than wear fur'. **Naomi Campbell** agrees, but later appears in American **magazine** W wearing a variety of pelts about her person. The fur industry has a lot of money to spend, and when Sophia Loren can be signed for a £2.2 million deal advertising the real thing, models find it hard to stick to their principles. In the past organizations like Lynx and later Respect for Animals have waged wars on the fur-buyers: 'It takes a hundred dumb animals to make a fur coat, and one to wear it' they proclaimed. Seventies superbeauty Marie Helvin swung a mink coat which sprayed blood as she moved in a David Bailey film accompanied by information about the appalling ways in which many animals were killed. Large animals were extinguished by inserting a red hot poker into the anus, so as not to damage the fur. Smaller animals like mink were skinned alive. The fur industry claims that no such atrocities continue, and justifies its continued existence as a result. Rising **New York** fashion designer Isaac Mizrahi is quoted as saying 'I'm feeling fur right now', while **Kristen McMenamy** models a **Christian Dior** coat with a large beaver collar. It's a contentious issue, and one that can no longer be blamed on bloated businessmen garnishing their wives with proof of prosperity. One fur outlet recently revealed that 75 per cent of their sales were direct to women customers.

future fashion
When the fashion industry looks to the future it usually concocts a vision of spacey **synthetic** serenity. In reality, with the help of technology and computer-aided design, **clothes** may be made by bonding fabric to the exact measurements of the customer, dispensing with outdated size systems. As the function and speed of the Internet improves, all shopping could take place on the screen. A team at Nottingham Trent University is designing a digital fashion store in which consumers can feed their own bodily measurements to the computer and access a replica in the clothes of their choice. In an environment where resources are precious, extremely durable, bio-degradeable and **environmentally aware** fabrics will come to the fore. We may have fewer clothes that last longer. For **models**, **casting** is shortly to become a thing of the past, as CD Roms beam the talking, moving image of the individual onto the screens of potential employers. Speculation that the live catwalk **show** could become a thing of the past began a few years ago when **Rifat Ozbek** produced a video package of his collection ideas with leading film-maker John Maybury. Future **fashion editors** might be able to sit at their desks and watch designer offerings without having to argue about seating arrangements, or backstage passes. There would be no need to dress up in full **Prada** battledress and trek across Europe and America. Now what would be the point in that?

galliano, john Born in Gibraltar in 1960, John Galliano has become one of Britain's most prestigious **fashion designers**; since graduating from Central St Martin's School of Art in 1984 he has won British Fashion Designer of the Year a record number of times. He is an exceptional talent, combining elaborate research of historical garments with a modern eye and perfect finish. He embodies the eccentric English designer even more than **Vivienne Westwood**, and in complete contrast to the many designer giants who wear **jeans** and **t-shirts** for press photos. Galliano's own clothing is every bit as inventive as his work. He recently chose to be photographed in Heidi plaits and striped pyjama trousers, a photo that was beamed around the world.

G is for Glamour. Models Shalom and Kate backstage at Chanel, waiting for the glamour process to begin. Soon these women will be transformed into gorgeous goddesses sending hordes of lensmen into photographic rapture.

Galliano's staging of **shows** has the fashion press falling over itself for tickets. Audiences have had to file through a wardrobe to see a rooftop scene where sailors perched amongst the chimneys and **supermodels** promenaded in pink flamenco dresses; during the British Fashion Awards, **models** planted in the audience performed poetry readings, delivered speeches and chatted amongst themselves in the aisles. John Galliano has the fashion world at his feet. He recently became the designer for the House of Givenchy, where he is responsible for *prêt à porter* and *haute couture* lines. But he remains shy, polite and overmodest to the point of delivering short, sometimes giggly answers to camera **interviews**. At an extravagant press launch in the mid-eighties one suited exec not in the know eyed the young (but already extremely famous and strangely attired) Mr Galliano with suspicion, and asked for credentials. Instead of standing on his dignity, Galliano simply replied 'I'm John from Wood Green.' Ah, if only there were more!

gaultier, jean-paul
Amongst my favourite fashion types is French designer Jean-Paul Gaultier, whose challenging and thought-provoking ideas around gender **uniforms** are fused with stylized and impish presentation. He is a skilled tailor who plays with image and costume to effect irreverent send-ups of fashion itself. Like many in his field, he showed promise early, and at fourteen presented mini-collections of **clothes** to his mother and grandmother. When he was seventeen, he sent sketches to Pierre Cardin and was invited to join the company. He set up his own company in 1977, aged just twenty-five. His **shows** use **models** surfacing through holes in the floor, or winding their way through the crowd on a **fake** grass catwalk. He mixes top models with pop performers, and often uses deliberately strange looking people to parade his clothes. He has used a variety of unusual sites, including a skating rink which offered various skidding and slipping opportunities for those on the ice. And then there was an old railway hangar which he filled with **synthetic** snow. All of us that night suffered stinging eyes and throats from the chemical fumes, and it is testament to his popularity that we all sat rooted

to our chairs. His fascination with popular culture infuses everything he does; he currently appears on our screens as an accomplished presenter. Of all the designers he is best qualified to say he knows his customers, since he can be found in the clubs with them, dancing the night away in his favourite tartan kilt.

ghauri, yasmeen

The only Asian woman to reach **supermodel** status so far, Yasmeen Ghauri was born in Montreal to a German mother and a Pakistani father. She was seventeen when she was stopped by a hairdresser and given the name of a **modelling agency**. Although her ambitions were to become a painter, she took snapshots to the local agency and was signed on the spot. During her first summer in the business she worked only occasionally. The next year (in 1989) she went to **Milan**, then **Paris** and there she became the latest super to join the crowd. In her mid-twenties, Yasmeen's appeal is her elegance and sophistication. She is first choice for *haute couture* shows as well as *prêt à porter*. Most Asian and Japanese women do not grow tall enough to be considered for catwalk work, and her uniqueness has been hard for her. In rare **interviews** she hints at a profession full of criticism and envy, and offers an insight when she says, 'I want to go back to school to take classes in management and set up my own business — a business that will have nothing whatsoever to do with fashion.'

gigli, romeo Trained as an architect, Romeo Gigli gave his first **show** in 1982 against a tide of power-dressing and padded shoulders, quietly presenting sensitive, almost antique-like, **clothes**. His appreciation of simplicity has been likened to the approach of **Japanese designers**, but there is a gentle romance to his work which sets him apart. Eroticism is lace on a bustier, and poetry and fantasy are achieved by sending models down the runway with dresses tinkling like Venetian glass beads. Bright lights and wham bam sound tracks do not figure in his shows — he even held a candlelit presentation at twilight to maximize the effect of his iridescent fabrics and spicy colours.

His is a distinctly personal path born out of a childhood surrounded by old and rare books (his family had been antique book dealers for generations). Today Romeo Gigli (whose cheaper line G Gigli was launched in 1991) takes inspiration from those musty yet majestically bound classics, and conjures a vision of romantic heroine. He tarnished his shiny crown for me somewhat when he said, 'It's part of my personality to make women feminine, fragile and soft.' Ah well!

glamour

Another fashion industry buzz word and one that is frequently employed to describe a desirable woman, the history of the word reveals much about the associations between female **beauty** and witchcraft. Jane Mills, author of *Womanwords*, finds the word has its roots in the old English 'gramayre', meaning grammar or learning. By the fifteenth century female learning fell under suspicion and 'gramayre' soon came to mean occult learning. Women were encouraged by priests and holy men to leave all knowledge well alone, lest they be accused of witchcraft. By the end of the fifteenth century glamour had come to mean solely a form of magic spell or charm. *Malleus Maleficarum*, published in Germany in 1486, became the witch-hunters' manual for three hundred years, and offered detailed examples of 'glamour' when unfortunate young men were dispossessed of their 'virile member'. Women were credited with the ability to magic away the penises of helpless young men and store them in secret places like birds' nests high up in the branches of tall trees. In the contemporary dictionary, a 'glamorous' individual is beautiful *and* smart; only the smallest trace of this word's original meaning remains.

gucci

Among the most influential of fashion houses and currently the most copied, the Gucci business proper was founded in 1922 by Guccio Gucci, who expanded his saddlery to sell exclusive leather products. As the company's reputation grew flagship stores were built in major Italian cities. Following the death of Gucci

Senior in 1953, ownership passed to the three sons, and the company expanded to include shoes, silk scarves and watches. In the sixties, stylish women of the day sported Gucci accessories, and the brand — symbolized by the equestrian stirrup designs — embodied ideals of class and aristocracy. But when grandson Paulo Gucci emerged from the boardroom after a fight with his father and cousin with blood streaming down his face, his picture was to find its way into every newspaper in the world. Jacqueline Kennedy Onassis, one of many fans, even sent a telegram asking what was going on. During the eighties family rivalry escalated and resulted in bitter quarrels, lawsuits and even a murder. At the turn of the decade, the firm logged its worst year of trading, with huge financial losses. 1990 may have been a bad time for the balance sheet, but it was also the year American designer Tom Ford joined the company as an anonymous backroom design assistant. Shortly after the last Gucci family member was bought out by Investcorp in 1993, the young Mr Ford was given a chance to revitalize the image of the company. It is he who has single handedly reinvented Gucci as a style leader, offering *prêt à porter* collections which have had British and American **fashion editors** knocking down doors.

hair Archaeological remains show that both men and women have always lavished attention on their locks. Ancient Egyptians invented the concept of hairdressing as we know it, while Europeans were living semi-wild with ragged hair, smelly **clothes** and mud-covered faces, the African élite were structuring great tiers of hair upon their heads. These were delicately perfumed with concealed balls of wax, which slowly melted throughout the day to surround the wearer with aromatic scent. Early religions invested much power in the Goddess and her hair; mother Goddesses like the Greek Isis and Cybele, as well as Kali from ancient Indian myth, were credited with the power to command the weather by braiding and releasing

H is for High Heels. Many designers have their shoes especially made to enhance their collections and for some like Vivienne Westwood, this is an excellent opportunity to make a creative statement in the footwear department.

their hair. Much later, in Europe, the Christian Church held strong opinions on the ability of a woman's hair to seduce and corrupt men's minds. Churchmen were also convinced **witches** could raise storms and demons by unbinding their hair. The association of female hair and magic gave rise to the compulsory shaving of nuns, who gave up their 'powers' to serve God. Accused witches had their heads shaved, some torturers favouring total shaving, and for men accused of witchcraft this involved the removal of chest hair — hence the expression 'making a clean breast of things'. Christian men were instructed to shear their hair and beards at regular dates, to proclaim honesty. One of these dates fell on Maundy Thursday, the day before Good Friday. This day is described in old texts as 'Shear Day'. Women were required to conceal or tie back loose hair and are also encouraged to cover their heads in many contemporary religious situations; in some faiths, total removal is still required by a woman after marriage.

Hair has also been used to make political statements. During the twenties women hacked off wispy tendrils and luxurious locks as the short bob became popular among a new generation of women fighting for the right to vote and rejecting old-fashioned dress codes. More recently punks have made a big thing of hair and political allegiance. And the **Afro** is one of the abiding images of sixties civil rights activism.

hamnett, katharine
Born Katharine Appleton in Kent in 1948, she attended Cheltenham Ladies College and later Central St Martin's School of Art, and became Ms Hamnett after her marriage to a graphic designer. A rare breed of politically aware clothes-maker, our herioine shall forever be known by the photograph of her and Margaret Thatcher snapped during a Downing Street reception. She is in a silk **t-shirt** with the banner headline '58% don't want Pershing', and the Prime Minister sports a blue two-piece and a look that says 'I can't read it, I haven't got my glasses with me.' T-shirt history was made, and myriad copies using her banner headline approach followed. She has been critical

of the **British** fashion industry's inability to compete with European standards, and was one of the first designers to show her collections abroad in **Paris**, and then **Milan**. Besides having plenty to say (she even launched a **magazine**, *Tomorrow*, which bravely tried to mix fashion and politics), she is one of the few who is **environmentally aware**; she withdrew part of her collection from a Milanese catwalk once she learned of the fabric's suspected polluting qualities. Hamnett is mistress of the provocative statement; she once described herself as 'a combination of threat and a Fortnum's hamper'. My own favourite is 'Women are the hunters, sex is power, and why shouldn't you use your sexuality to ensnare [men] to obscure their judgement?' Why indeed!

haute couture

French words of course, which roughly translated mean 'high quality needlework'. We understand it as high fashion with bells on. Couturiers are **fashion designers** who rely on the skills of a variety of specialist craftspeople and use **labour**-intensive effects. Art historians tell of women in the 1800s who wore **clothes** made from priceless medieval tapestries, and even their shoe-trees were fashioned out of the finest antique violins. When these women sat for their portraits in their Cartier diamonds, grand couturiers like **Worth** would create gowns especially for the occasion. In 1858 **Charles Frederick Worth** hit upon the idea of a fashion show to present his garments to royal buyers. *Haute couture* is now an industry protected by law, the main criteria were set in 1945 and updated in 1992. Regulations include size of business and number of collections presented. There are eighteen *haute couture* houses in France, employing four thousand, five hundred people with a turnover of around $1 billion.

Since the growth of ***prêt à porter*** (ready to wear), emphasis on exclusivity and cost has waned. The fifties saw the demise of many couture houses, and those that survive today have embraced the importance of marketing and reputation to attract fresh interest. Many exhibit their couture designs at **shows** during the months of

January and July. Press and **fashion buyers** attend these, but the world's media do not give the same space to the clothes in their publication or programming as to *prêt à porter*. These couture clothes are aimed at a very select few. Individual clients are often treated to private shows and expect attention and fitting sessions from the designers themselves. In **Versace**'s Atelier couture range, prices start at £10,000. The garments are made to fit the exact bodily measurements of these wealthy women who spend thousands, even millions, each season. Only two thousand women buy *haute couture*, and the future for such an élitist industry relies heavily on the ability of its masters (there are few top women offering this service) to entice a younger, independently successful breed of consumer. Givenchy's recruitment of **John Galliano** hints at such a strategy.

H is for *Haute Couture*. Elaborate and expensive clothes can cost their owners tens of thousands of pounds. Here Christy Turlington wears a modest number from Christian Dior.

high heels On the catwalk, a six-foot **model** in high heels can become a towering giantess, regal, formidable and impressive. Designers – masters of artifice and subterfuge – employ all sorts of tricks to create a look of power and potency. High heels are an example of **fetish** wear that has become standard attire for women. Since the fifties, when **Dior**'s **New Look** incorporated high heels as must-have **footwear**, high street versions of this fetish shoe have enjoyed popularity. Our mothers wore them all day, and while some women can proudly report running for buses, they can also show a variety of bunions, corns and deformed toes. Eighty per cent of visitors to the chiropodist are women with problems caused by ill-fitting footwear. Apart from obvious damage to **feet**, high heels have been shown to interfere with the natural position of the pelvis, forcing the spine to take extra strain. Women who wear high heels often can experience a shortening of the

muscles at the back of the leg, making walking in bare feet painful. Yet the desire to own a pair of heels is still strong, and little girls throughout the land practise in their mothers' cast-offs, or even their own trainer heels.

The spiked heel is symbolic of pain and power, pleasure and punishment. Women in fetishistic publications are frequently depicted in shoes too high and restrictive to be comfortable or practical. Toe cleavage, where the mouth of the shoe is cut lower to display tops of toes squashed into the covered area, is thought by some to be extremely erotic. The power of the wearer is assumed to be in her ability to dominate those aroused by the sight of the foot crammed into the shoe. Some even fantasize about the pain inflicted by the spike, should its wearer become displeased. Over the years a single image of the high heel has come to represent sexual woman.

historical clothing Many designers – **Vivienne Westwood** being

one of the most prominent – love to visit the past and offer romantic reconstructions of clothing from bygone times. Britain has a long history of textile-making and early records show that it was women who were largely responsible for the production of clothing. At this time **clothes** for both men and women were based on a simple t-shaped shift. Gender differences were marked by the treatment of the head – women concealed their **hair**. By the mid-1300s, as trading links strengthened, male-dominated textile guilds emerged, along with systems of apprenticeships for weavers, cloth-cutters and tailors. Women quickly became excluded from this growing trade, and around the same time England became inspired by the clothing of the French court. Ideas of fashion rather than function began to take hold, and men and women invested clothing with the ability to do much more than protect from the elements. Historians have linked the first period of significant fashion change with the rise of mercantile Europe in the mid-1400s. A broader choice of goods from traders, and a speeding-up of ideas and styles, produced an environment now identified as 'the birth of modern fashion'. Now gender and social roles were more clearly defined by garments. The expansion of the English textile industry was helped by investment from foreign sources such as Florentine bankers. By the mid-1500s **London** was well established as a fashionable centre attracting visitors and traders. Free enterprise grew, and all who could afford to buy rich fabrics like silks and velvets adorned themselves with pride; individual and newly acquired style could not be differentiated from upper-class wealth. Church and government, worried that nobility and market traders were indistinguishable, introduced the 1533 Sumptuary Laws in an attempt to curb over-zealous fashion consumption. Grooms and servants could only wear cheap woollen cloth, merchants worth £1000 were permitted to dress no better than gentlemen, while knights could dress as they pleased, excluding ermine. These were ignored until 1566, when the first fashion police were posted on the gates of London, these Renaissance bouncers barred entry to the city with their equivalent of 'You can't come in here looking like that, mate.'

The 1700s saw the beginning of unprecedented industrial expansion, as the textile and clothing industry was geared up to supply in mass and at speed. Fashion was fast becoming available to a much wider group of consumers. The consumer revolution, with the help of expanding **retail** and **magazine** trades, was about to begin!

hobble skirt
Introduced by Paul Poiret just after the turn of the century, this new style allowed for only the smallest of steps to be taken. The skirt, cut and draped to narrow severely at a point between the knee and ankle, was satirized – and even denounced by the Pope. The very act of walking was so comical and laborious that travel on foot became impossible. Female scholars of the day noted with irony how such a style could become popular at a time when marches of female protesters and suffragettes were just getting into their stride. As with modernday styles like **Baby Doll** fashions, the wearers may have been subconsciously reassuring their oppressors that there was nothing to worry about, really. Small mincing steps then, as opposed to giant strides on behalf of womankind.

Après-show, camera crews swarm backstage like locusts, hunting down an interview with the newest model, the hairdresser, the milliner, celebrity guests, the designer, even the designer's mother. Look in on the same scene moments later when the mob have moved to the next show and the aftermath will resemble a small town hit by a tornado.

interviews During the show season, television journos are operating on high-octane anxiety, under orders to secure at all costs a soundbite from each **fashion designer** after their catwalk presentation. Getting backstage in **Paris**, for instance, involves negotiating various bouncers and **public relations** types in an attempt to bring back the bounty. Once you've run this gauntlet, the designer can usually be located by the surrounding cast of marvellously groomed supporters, bright lights, home-team camera crews and lines of journalists anxiously waiting their moment. Interviews are not always well organized, and this is a tense moment for any frock hack. Attempting to grab an interview between hordes of immaculately coiffed followers and an entourage of hangers-on is just like being a stranger at a crowded party where everyone is too hip to talk. The pressure to bag some chat and move on quickly mounts, as there is precious little time to relocate to the next show. With a camera permanently rolling and a mike outstretched, those of us who attempt to introduce the mike with subtlety and a knowledgeable question do not fare any better than those who butt in with indifference. In my time I have been kissed mid-question by a flirtatious **J-P Gaultier**, suggestively squeezed by a passer-by while interrogating **Karl Lagerfeld** and shoved violently to one side by a German radio reporter during an intense bout of jostling for **Rifat**. While journalistic skills have helped, the ability to scrum without damaging my favourite John Richmond jacket has stood me in even better stead.

A designer cluster! From left to right: Bruce Oldfield, Vivienne Westwood, Gianni Versace, John Galliano, Rifat Ozbeck

jackson, betty Born in 1940 in Backup, Lancashire, Betty Jackson is one of the **British** design nobility. She has even received an MBE for her services to British industry and exports. After graduating from Birmingham College of Art in 1971, having studied **textile design** as well as fashion, Ms Jackson began as an illustrator and then worked as the chief designer for the Quorum label. In 1981 she set up her own company, launched with her husband and business partner David Cohen. She specialized in separates, rescaled to sometimes larger proportions to give a loose, floppy and highly wearable feel, and featured textile prints as part of her look. In 1985, she won British Fashion Council Designer of the Year, and more recently took up a post as consultant to Marks and Spencer.

J is for Japanese design. The work of Issey Miyake featuring his signature pleats.

The customer is what matters to this designer, who after her runway shows makes an elegant appearance with her walking stick. She is warm and approachable – 'I've often said hello to people in the street when all I recognize is their clothes' – and remains one of the most 'ordinary-woman' friendly designers, combining easy style with comfort. 'We have some brilliant designers in the UK,' she says, 'but unless they are designing for the women in the street, they are not doing their job.' Here, here.

japanese designers
While **Issey Miyake** is the best known Japanese designer on the international circuit, Yohji Yamamoto and Rei Kawakubo of Comme des Garçons have also made a big impact on western fashion design, with their minimalist styling and frugal designs, often in black or dark colours. Yamamoto and Kawakubo graduated from Keio University in Tokyo with academic qualifications before exploring fashion. Separately, but with similar approach, they deliver a design philosophy that structures cloth and texture around the body, creating a disciplined, sombre and aloof effect, the antithesis of the vroom-vroom pussy-pelmet and push-up bra types. Kenzo, the son of hotel-keepers, opened his boutique in the early seventies and named it Jungle Jap. A free spirit, energetic and adventurous, he showed his first winter collection made entirely from quilted cotton (due to lack of money), and from there amassed a large following in America.
London-based Michiko Koshino, the youngest of a talented trio of sisters who are all established designers, sells to Japan and Korea and capitalizes on her London **streetstyle** image. In her shows a variety of clubland figures mix with models to a riot of music and colour. She was the first designer to market condoms under her own name, and besides operating 35 licences ranging from watches to car interiors, she currently presides over plans to open a series of fashion superstores in Hong Kong.

jeans
From the French *Genes* for Genoa, the Italian port where sailors in the 1800s wore sturdy work pants, blue jeans are the utility item of the twentieth

century. Not necessarily cheap, often drab and sometimes uncomfortable, a clue to the durability of jeans might be found in their ability to adapt to seasonal trends over the decades, and individual wearer requirements. Youth movements of every kind utilize the jean, customizing and augmenting this basic workwear item with considerable ingenuity. In the UK alone, 50 million pairs are sold each year. In a fiercely competitive market, worth £1,292 million, jeans companies employ **advertising** agencies to spread brand awareness. Levi dominates the UK market, with 71 per cent of those questioned opting for this company as the leader. Nearest rivals are Wrangler with 9 per cent and Lee with 3 per cent. Other brands at around 1 per cent are Falmer, Lee Cooper, Pepe and Marco Polo. Jeans advertising frequently evokes images of the good old West, featuring durability and close-to-the-earth, workwear classic appeal. Standard hip-today has-been tomorrow connotations do not fit well with an item of clothing that hasn't changed from its original design, a century ago. Faces from the fashion world lend their bodies to campaigns: Paula Abbot featured in Wrangler's 'Ranching Out' campaign, and Levi's used space babe Kristina Semenovskaia, cutting-edge technology and a now legendary soundtrack to conjure a future where Levi 501 is standard inter-galactic attire. The pressure to present a winning composition of situation, role model and overall image is strong. When Levi hit the jackpot with singer Nick Kamen and their now infamous 'Launderette' ad in the early eighties, sales of 501s were boosted by 800 per cent. Of all the pairs of jeans bought in Britain each year, 2 per cent are made by Joe Bloggs, a British jeans company run by Shami Ahmed. Begun in the mid-eighties, and situated in Manchester, this company exploded from a street-market stall in Lancashire to become a household name. In an environment where big-name designers compete for a slice of the jeans action, press stunts and clever marketing ideas are all. In a move to out-**Versace** Versace, Joe Bloggs produced diamond-encrusted jeans worth £150,000 worn by various TV personalities at trade fairs. The world's most expensive jeans are currently kept in a safe.

karan, donna In just a decade and a half, Donna Karan, born in New York in 1948, has worked her way up from the rag trade to designer celebrity by 'making black appropriate to every occasion'. Daughter of a fashion **model** and a haberdasher, and now head of a corporation predicted to turnover $1 billion by the year 2000, Ms Karan and her husband Stephan Weiss manage a company that employs 1600 people and produces women's and **menswear**, **children's clothes**, accessories, skin care, and the DKNY range. Her image is of a no-nonsense career woman who has made a fortune out of America's penchant for power dressing; in reality she is a soft-centre with hippy tendencies. During a recent collection, she

K is for Knitwear. A new generation of knitwear designers attempt to inject excitement into knitted clothes. Royal College of Art graduate Julian McDonald now designs for a variety of top fashion houses, including Chanel.

personally brushed the seats of top **fashion editors** with rosemary and sage, 'to soften their cynical natures'.

klein, calvin
Born in **New York** in 1942, Calvin Klein taught himself to sew and draw as a child, and went on to graduate from the Fashion Institute of Technology in 1962. He worked as an apprentice at the Seventh Avenue coat and suit house by day, while creating his own portfolio in the evenings. He started Calvin Klein Ltd in 1968 with his long-time friend Barry Schwartz and a loan of $2,000. He specialized in designing coats and suits, and in 1973 was the youngest designer ever to win the American Coty Award. Today his empire includes **sportswear**, **underwear**, **furs**, bed linens, cosmetics and fragrances. Calvin Klein Home, a luxury home furnishings collection, was introduced in April 1995. Considered the foremost exponent of pared-down style, he has said 'It is important not to confuse simplicity with uninteresting.' Just in case there is anyone out there thinking the latter (and in my mind it's easy to), he provides a complementary advertising experience which at times, has commanded the full attention of the western world! In the eighties a fifteen-year-old Brooke Shields proclaimed, 'You know what comes between me and my Calvins? Nothing.' Later **Kate Moss**, childlike, thin and naked, drapes herself across a sofa under the headline 'Obsession for Men'. Complaints followed and the ads were dropped. Still later the FBI investigated a series of television, **magazine** and billboard ads which contained underage models in states of undress. Mr Klein defended his penchant for **Lolita** types with a full-page ad in the *New York Times* claiming they were meant to convey 'the spirit, independence and inner worth of today's young people'. His fragrances, Obsession, Eternity and Escape, are among the best marketed smells in the world, and his latest perfume CK1, launched in 1994, was inspired he says by his daughter Marci (who it is reported survived a kidnap attempt). Klein was clearly unaffected by the disapproval of the moral majority and his bland brand/porny images was clearly a winning combination. Klein continued to climb. In 1993 the Council of Fashion Designers of

America voted him Outstanding Designer of the Year for both womenswear and **menswear**, making him the first designer ever to receive both distinctions concurrently.

knitwear

knitwear A less glamorous division of the fashion design industry; but designers like Artwork – owned and run by husband and wife team Jane and Patrick Gotelier – and Rena de Prato, have built businesses offering knitted garments that mirror styles and themes on the catwalk. Technical innovations such as computerized knitting machines have afforded exciting developments, and some colleges offer specialist courses. Certain trends have evolved around knitted items themselves. **Coco Chanel** designed the original twinset, a two-piece knitted cardigan and undergarment, as part of a campaign to furnish women with easy elegance. Otto Weiss conceived the name 'twinset' and marketed it as a desirable commodity in 1937 while working for Pringle. Knitwear lends itself well to *trompe-l'oeil* effects, and in the thirties **Elsa Schiaparelli** set the trend by designing sweaters with collars knitted in as part of the design. Today the biggest creative force on the international knitwear front is Missoni, run by another husband and wife team Rosita and Tai Missoni, who met in 1948 when Rosita was studying English and Tai was competing with the Italian Olympic track team. He was a manufacturer of tracksuits and she worked for her parents' bedspread manufacturing company. When they bought four knitting machines in 1953 and began to craft innovative designs with relief-patterned geometric shapes they caused a huge stir. Their skills are celebrated in fine art galleries as well as on the catwalk, where they have recently enjoyed a big revival as current focus on **Milan** continues.

labour As fashion is democratized and the choice of styles in our high streets has never been greater, price has never been more important. In Britain many of our popular stores keep their prices down at the expense of workers. **British** sweatshops are a reality; workers labour in unsafe, poorly lit, badly heated cramped conditions; their wages are staggeringly low, and they have no rights. Jobs are not registered, since often employees are without legal citizenship. Homeworkers – often women – are also used as cheap labour, recruited spasmodically when fluctuations in orders require extra deliveries to be fulfilled. In developing countries human beings are treated as an inexhaustible resource.

L is for London. In the early eighties, London exploded into life and young designers hit the headlines; today the genius of newcomer Alexander McQueen is watched by the world's press.

Despite label declarations which state one country of origin, a global assembly line may mean the final garment is the result of a combined effort from workers of several countries. Countries in Asia and South America operate free trade zones which enjoy exemption from labour laws. This facilitates government-sanctioned abuse of workers in pursuit of profit. It is estimated that 85 per cent of the employees in free trade zones are young women, and half of these are employed in textile and garment production. Trade unions are banned and brutal policing is used to enforce regulations. Girls as young as twelve are expected to work extremely long hours seven days a week, sleeping on the factory floor.

Despite these facts, many of our own well-known stores choose to sidestep the ethics, placing orders through agents without researching source factories or procedures. Subcontracting chains are a popular way in which 'respectable' companies can keep their hands clean. 'Clean **clothes**' campaigns offer two main courses of action: consumers can refuse to buy from high street stores which collaborate with oppressive regimes or condone the existence of British sweatshops; or we can buy clothes that have been humanely produced to start with, giving our business to the many small companies who operate fair trade policies with workers all over the world.

lacroix, christian
Born in 1951, Christian Lacroix is credited for revitalizing *haute couture* by injecting a much-needed sense of humour and a high-fashion approach. He is someone who values the cloth, often reawakening old industries and forgotten methods of production involving the manual skill of craftspeople. His ready to wear collection is often the most extravagant visual feast of fabric and colour on the French fashion calendar. He owes his interest in fashion to his childhood in Provence, where he was surrounded by female family members who made **clothes**. At university he studied art history, ancient Greek and Latin. He then worked as a museum curator before becoming design assistant at Hermes and

later chief designer at Patou. In 1987, backed by a French conglomerate that also owns **Dior**, be began designing under his own name – and was an instant success.

lagerfeld, karl
Born in Hamburg, Germany in 1938, young Lagerfeld was sent to **Paris** at fourteen to further his studies. At seventeen, after winning a coat design competition sponsored by the International Wool Secretariat, he was hired by couturier Balmain. He remained there for three years and moved to Patou at just twenty years old. A veteran by the time he was in his mid-twenties, Karl called it a day and packed his bags to study art history in Italy. He returned to clothing couture the following year in 1969 and began a highly productive period of freelance design with various companies including Chloe, Krizia and Fendi. In 1983 he became design director of **Chanel**, and in 1984 he launched his first collection under his own name. He is amongst the most prolific of designers, and besides designing **fur** and **sportswear** lines for Fendi, he has revitalized the House of Chanel by customizing the famous Chanel two piece suit, combining salon style sophistication with hip hop and surfing **streetstyles**. He doesn't enjoy the same press adulation for his own label designs and has a reputation for grandiose gestures. When not consulted for the Hollywood film *Prêt à Porter*, he withdrew and later sought a ban on the film. He has also been known to criticize designers for their tendency to think too much about themselves and not enough about their collections.

With his signature fan and ponytail, Karl Lagerfeld can frequently be found backstage after a show entertaining international **fashion editors** and **fashion buyers** in several different languages, and of all the designer luvvies, he is the one who clocks up the longest post-**show** appearance. Long after the room has been evacuated of dressers, **models**, crews and hangers on, he is still locked in conversation, happy to talk to students about his latest works.

lang, helmut

One of the few Viennese names to have a large presence in the fashion world, Lang was raised in the Austrian Alps and studied business before turning his hand to clothing design. For some time he has pioneered sombre minimalism against a backdrop of dressy **glamour**, and has therefore enjoyed a mixed reception. I prefer functional practicality to bosomy splendour any day, but I still wonder why sad **waif** models in plain shifts are interesting. Lang's fans are a powerful bunch, however, and with the current vogue for simplicity Helmut Lang has explored a serene mix of understatement, modernity and **synthetic** fabric.

laundering

A revolution in modern textiles has quietly taken place. High fashion and washing machines do not mix. Most of us entrust our favourite **clothes** to the dry cleaners, and even cheap high street items reveal annoying 'Dry clean only' instructions. This may cut down on laundry time, but it means that the washing machine has been demoted. For centuries women laboured with cast iron cauldrons and crude soaps, then French chemists discovered a means of making soda (the necessary alkaline) from salt. In England William Hesketh Lever – later Lord Leverhulme – marketed soap with attractive packaging and **advertising** – a forerunner of today's 'doorstep challenge'. For a long time clothes-washing was the province of servants, so not much stress was put on finding **labour**-saving devices. Despite numerous experiments with various washing contraptions, it was not until after the First World War that a small percentage of homes could boast basic industrialization in the laundry department.

Today we have returned to historical methods of laundering – paying others to clean our clothes for us. This time, however, we accept the use of noxious chemicals as part of the process. The majority of dry cleaners use the chlorinated chemical perchloroethylene, known as perc. It is vented into the air from shops and carried into our homes on the clothes. In the USA perc is listed by the Environmental Protection Agency as a hazardous air pollutant. Californian shops have to display this sign: 'This store dry cleans garments with perchloroethylene, a chemical known in the state of California to cause cancer. This chemical is present in the air in the store. A residue of the chemical remains in dry cleaned garments and passes into surrounding air for several days.' Greenpeace maintain that studies have linked this chemical to miscarriages amongst dry cleaning workers. Perc also breaks down into toxic pollutants linked to forest decline and contaminated ground water. However, there are dry cleaners who now use Aquatex; a new wet cleaning system which uses soap and water in computer controlled amounts. Even suede and leather can be cleaned without the use of nasty substances. So when it comes to toxic chemicals, just say no.

lauren, ralph

Born Ralph Lipschitz in New York in 1939, the young Mr Lipschitz worked as a glove salesman while attending night school for business studies. In 1967 he joined Beau Brummel Neckwear, and created the Polo Division to produce wide handmade expensive neckties as he continued to experiment with men's clothing, later introducing the Polo range. Lauren reckoned Americans wanted branding rather than designer names. He chose the polo player because it evoked 'sophisticated sport' and 'stylish people'. The Ralph Lauren womenswear range was launched in 1972 using luxury fabrics like cashmere and tweed to create an understated elegance with English undertones. His success is due to fusing marketing nous with innate American desire for heritage; he has been called the 'pioneer of lifestyle advertising' and the 'Godfather of fashion marketing'. His personal fortune is calculated at between $500 million and $700 million, and his empire is estimated at $4.4 billion. Ralph Lauren is a progressive thinker on many fronts; he has been instrumental in a recent charity initiative called Fashion Targets Breast Cancer in which he galvanized the entire American fashion industry to raise funds and awareness on the subject of breast cancer.

lolita Nabokov's Lolita is a true heroine to the fashion industry, selling concepts of everlasting youth with serene cunning; most of the time we aren't aware of the way in which our anxieties around ageing are nurtured and manipulated. Recent attempts to justify the need for young girls (as young as twelve) to don full **make-up**, slinky **clothes** and flirt with the camera would be laughable if they weren't so pathetic. The schoolgirl in question was five foot ten inches tall, with a yearning for **modelling** stardom. Just as the likes of **Kate Moss** and other women in their late teens were required to act and dress as though years older, now pre-pubescents with undeveloped bodies are posing as stand-ins for eighteen year olds. The male photographer who worked with her on her first shoot did not want an older woman, he wanted a young girl pretending to be an older woman. There is, of course, a world of difference between a woman who is old enough to behave like a sexually mature adult, making choices based on experience and accrued wisdom, and a girl who, with the encouragement of make-up artists, **stylists** and **fashion photographers**, can dress up and pretend to look like all of the above.

london The smallest of the four events on the fashion calendar, London Fashion Week is nevertheless extremely important to press and **fashion buyers** looking for innovation and adventure. With a plethora of young **fashion designers** showing, the media is guaranteed a news story. The meet takes place in the grounds of the Natural History Museum in early autumn and early spring. Around thirty designers show their collections, most from two huge and very grand tents with catwalks inside. The event takes months of coordination, as most of these **shows** are fitted into a four-day programme.

lipstick In Europe after the First World War, the need for women to present an attractive and desirable appearance was paramount now that there was only one man for every three to four women. As women ditched post-Victorian dress codes and experimented with loose, even masculine, clothing, **make-up** also performed a vital role in restating gender differences. American Maurice Levy invented the modern lipstick in 1915, and soon round, pouting lips, epitomized by the ultimate flapper of the day Clara Bow, could be easily applied to any **face**. Just as a flower draws insects to its centre by means of distinctive markings, so the full and fleshy red lips lure the eyes to the most sexually charged feature on the face.

A generation of full-lipped Hollywood actresses engaged in dramatic screen kissing sequences, and the idea that lipsticked lips were more kissable engendered a trend in flavoured shades. Women became inseparable from their lippie. Navy nurses evacuated from submarines during the Second World War even included lipstick amongst the few personal items they took with them.

In the fifties, as society searched for the ultimate woman — sex siren and home-maker rolled into one — Dorothy Gray of **London** introduced 'pink mink' to 'go with anything'. In the sixties, women wore **baby-doll** clothes, and pale or pastel lips made mouths look child-like and unthreatening. In the eighties, a mainstream tendency towards achievement in the workplace produced bold but distinctly matt and unglossy reds and brick colours. In our free time we experimented with femininity, pleasing ourselves in punky blues or yellows.

magazines Glossy fashion magazines are put together many months in advance of the date they eventually reach the news-stands. **Fashion shoots** are planned meticulously and require a team of **fashion editors**, **stylists** and junior assistants to decide on themes and collect **clothes** from the designers' **public relations** officers (or PRs), while top **fashion photographers** are lured to add prestige to the proceedings. Some photographers insist on working with their own team of **models**, **make-up** and **hair** artists. Often a **casting** will take place, as models with portfolios arrive to be chosen from a large crowd sent by various

M is for Menswear. Adventurous menswear designers like Jean-Paul Gaultier try to introduce feminine elements to masculine dressing. Naturally this offers a provocative photo opportunity, but in reality few mainstream men are comfortable enough with their femininity to copy the styles or buy the clothes.

model agencies. Once the shoot (featuring the following season's clothes) is completed a fashion editor will select key transparencies. The fashion junior will contact the PR for a list of prices and retail outlets for the clothes featured. The slides or prints will then be handed to an art director who controls the finished design of the publication right down to choosing the typeface for each feature. All magazines have a house style, their own particular look. A flat plan of every page of the magazine is drawn and features are planned around advertising campaigns, which are given prime sites within the magazine. The pressure to get each issue looking good is high, as the costs of a top class fashion magazine – which must be met by the advertising budget – can mount to half a million pounds!

It was around the 1700s, when the idea of fashion as a national industry began to emerge, that fashion journals were created to highlight the latest styles and the finer points of postural finesse, with the English *The Lady's Magazine* leading the field. In 1794 Niklaus Wilhelm von Heideloff from Stuttgart produced *The Gallery of Fashion*. To this day his intricately engraved plates, displaying fully accessorized figures with accompanying captions, are highly prized by collectors. Later Samuel Beeton (husband of Mrs Beeton) lauched *The Queen* and *The English Woman's Domestic Magazine*. Now that the retail sector was expanding to accommodate a growing ready to wear or *prêt à porter* market, access to fashionable clothing was enjoyed by more women. Beauty parlours were beginning to crop up, and the idea that feminine appearance needed to be monitored and written about began to take shape. Fashionable clothing and the beautifying process were marketed as skills to be learned. Make-up especially became the subject of considerable discussion. Etiquette dictated a need for correct behaviour at all times, and this included the appropriate application of cosmetics. One writer advised rouge sticks and powder puffs for going out to lunch but not to dinner; another decreed that only married women might use it. British *Vogue* was launched in 1916. Advertisers were quick to spot an opportunity to reach a group of women anxious to maintain respectability and fashionable appearance. Expensive glossies originally targeted middle-class women, and then in the 1920s and 1930s, *Woman's Own*, *Woman* and *Good Housekeeping* emerged to cater for readers with less cash. Now cultural dictates of the day could be imparted with maximum effectiveness to a larger audience. Beauty competitions became popular and the make-up industry blossomed. Magazines began to act as market researchers, helping advertisers to market their products more efficiently. After the Second World War, advertising expenditure increased dramatically as companies competed for a bigger slice of postwar prosperity. This in turn meant magazines could afford to spend more on presentation and production.

Today, with a deluge of glossies to choose from, each one packed to the gills with advice and information about body and **face** maintenance, we often read the same message over and over again. Mainstream magazines convey a standard image of feminine appearance and provide instructions on how to achieve it. Cosmetics companies allocate fortunes to advertise their products, competing for prime sites requiring extra premiums. Beauty editors are under particular – if unspoken – pressure to endorse advertised products in their editorial; some large companies will not designate yearly budgets (vital for a magazine's continued existence and important attractions for other potential advertisers) without guarantees of complimentary features. Many writers find themselves in the position of having to sanction merchandise they personally dislike.

make-up Anthropologists believe that early cosmetics may have been formulated to protect the wearer from insects or extreme weather conditions. Certainly the wide variety of sweet-smelling pots containing animal fats and perfumed resin found in the tomb of Tutankhamen suggest a sophisticated understanding of cosmetic preparations. In fact there is even evidence to suggest that cosmetics were used over nine thousand years before the reign of the

Egyptian Boy Emperor. At first bodies and **faces** may have been decorated and protected with coloured clays, later malachite green paste was used to protect the eyes against light, and soon became prized for its decorative qualities.

In England, it was not until the twelfth century, when traders returned from the East with perfumed oils and dyes for lips and eyes, that the idea of artificially applied colour and skin decoration for fashionable purposes was introduced. By the time of Queen Elizabeth I women especially were smitten, and regularly applied a whole range of dubious substances to their faces. Sublimate of mercury was a popular extract for removing freckles, and when applied, the outer layer of skin would fall away from the face like damp wallpaper, leaving the lower layer of raw and corroded flesh perfectly freckle free. Ceruse, favoured as a skin whitener until the nineteenth century, was composed of lead oxide, hydroxide and carbonate. This deadly poisonous concoction was mixed on a palette with egg white and sometimes vinegar, then applied to the skin as a paste with a damp cloth. To fix the look, a little shellac varnish might be brushed over the whole face to create the perfect toxic face pack effect. Fucus, an early **lipstick** containing mercuric sulphide which stained lips red, had the desired effect for pouting princesses, but it also killed them. Many privileged women died young as these cumulative poisons were gradually absorbed and built up in the body. **Beauty** on the breadline however, meant that village girls had to be content with substitutes such as cornflour or borax for whitening their ruddy complexions and cochineal or berries for colouring cheeks and lips. Naturally these young women lived considerably longer.

In 1770, during a period of spectacular misogyny embodied in witchhunts, an Act of parliament was passed which threatened various penalties (including death in some cases) for women engaging in ritualistic practices involving face painting and the application of 'beauty aids':

Whatever age, rank, profession or degree, whether virgins, maids or widows that shall impose upon, seduce and betray into matrimony any of His Majesty's subjects by the scents, paints, cosmetic washes, artificial teeth, false hair, Spanish Wool, iron stays, hoops, high-heeled shoes, bolstered hips, upon conviction, the marriage shall be null and void.

The law was unenforceable, but **British** women weren't taking any chances. For the next century or so anything other than a dash of soap and water was beyond the pale. The early modern cosmetics pioneers had to navigate this difficult terrain with care. They marketed their products as faintly medicinal, performing a natural function rather than a beautifying one. At the end of Queen Victoria's reign, Helena Rubinstein tentatively ventured forth with a Valaze cream for healing spots, and the company Cheeseborough Ponds developed the popularity of the Ponds' Extract Cream by describing it as being good for constipation, colds, hayfever, malarial fever, syphilis and typhoid.

After the First World War, however, make-up became an important accessory for a generation of women who had worked in the munitions factories and now had money to spend. As if anxious to reassure everyone including themselves that their femininity was still intact despite having done men's work, women set about painting their faces with enthusiasm. The fully made-up face soon became the sign of the worker — upper-class women used make-up with more restraint. By the 1930s accentuated and colourful lips with painted eyebrows were once again the rage, as women looked to Hollywood for feminine role models. Actresses such as Jean Harlow and Joan Crawford used dramatic make-up effects to enhance their image. The airbrushed studio publicity pictures promoting these starlets presented a mask-like vision of untouchable cool. By the fifties sophisticated **advertising** and marketing techniques turned the cosmetics industry into a land of giants. Charles Revson of Revlon was one of the biggest operators. Faces became defined in line with the sculpted fashions of the **New Look**, and as more women attempted to join the work force, surveys of the day noted that those who worked out of the house bought and wore more make-up than women working at home as mothers and housewives. Ordinary women began to feel undressed without cosmetics. Revlon began to bring out a new colour every season to coincide with the fashion calendar and the interests of the cosmetics and fashion industries merged and enhanced one another.

male models
When Swedish supermale Marcus Schenkenberg stepped on to the largest catwalk in Europe at the Birmingham NEC at the *Clothes Show Live*, he was the most famous male model in the world. His torso first shot to fame in a **Calvin Klein** ad, and his rugged good looks and shoulder-length **hair** have since placed him in a similar earning bracket to his **supermodelling** sisters. He did not, however, draw the huge applause Naomi and Karen Moulder had enjoyed in years before, and this peeved him slightly. Despite producing his own calendar, as well as **modelling** for some of the world's top designers, his **face** is hardly known by mainstream audiences. Men do not enjoy the same power and status in this particular career as women. This happens for obvious reasons; **menswear** shows do not enjoy the same press interest; the male **fragrance industry** is considerably smaller than the female equivalent; and cosmetics and **beauty** industry imagery is almost exclusively feminine.

Nonetheless, there has been huge growth in male model imagery, largely fuelled by the explosion in men's style **magazines**. **Model agencies** insist that the stereotypical image of square-jawed beefcake is outdated, and a whole spate of imagery featuring delicate and fine-bone beauties, led by **British**-born Keith Martin, have infiltrated our glossies. Male models are not prized for their youthful faces and bodies in quite the same way women are, and many don't begin modelling until their twenties. Albert Delegue, who recently died just a few days short of his thirty-second birthday, was still at the top of his career, selling everything from **Giorgio Armani** aftershave to Marks and Spencer shorts. Male models do have to contend with a variety of adversaries, however, usually in the shape of footballers and actors who make guest appearances in **advertising** campaigns to promote an ideal of ordinary blokishness as opposed to the perceived vain and manicured masculinity of the modelling fraternity.

Black male models are frequently portrayed as mean and moody, freakish, or overtly sexual, required more often than their white colleagues to wear less clothing down the runway. So far ad agencies and clients are restricted by a racial myopia that assumes young Caucasians do not respond to black role models. But where African American and black British men are allowed to excel, they do, and young males up and down the country worship the achievements of their black sporting heroes. It naturally follows that black male models can have the same impact in the fashion world, if they were allowed access. **Ralph Lauren** recently contracted Tyson Beckford, now reputed to be amongst the highest paid male models in the world. The suspicion that Beckford was only recruited in line with the increasing popularity of Lauren's clothing among young African Americans serves as confirmation yet again that the fashion industry – despite its claims – is following trends rather than leading them.

mcmenamy, kristen

I like Kristen. I like the fact that in the **modelling** world she supposedly flies the flag on behalf of 'ugly' women everywhere. She has been known to liken herself to a martian drug addict. She was with a top **model agency** but clients were not requesting her. Then she shaved her eyebrows off and cut her **hair** and has worked continuously, with top **fashion photographers** like Stephen Meisel, Herb Ritts and Richard Avedon, ever since. At five feet ten inches, with red hair and blue eyes, elegant bone structure and full lips, this graceful woman is hardly an eyesore. True, she does not look like a **Barbie** doll, and she even inspired a letter to American *Vogue* from a reader who found her frightening. Such a response is a revealing insight into the fashion world's mass production of vacuous and unthreatening beauty. More please, Kristen.

mcqueen, alexander

The most talented **British** designer to emerge for some time. Son of a cab driver, McQueen who left school at sixteen marries exquisite tailoring skills with hard-edged **streetstyle** to create a vision that has fashion cognoscenti either beside themselves with excitement or slating his unsettling presentation of femininity and costume. He began by working for Savile Row tailors Anderson and Shepherd, later for Gieves and Hawkes, and then theatrical costumiers Bermans and Nathans. After nine months with **Romeo Gigli** and an MA at Central St Martin's School of Art, he launched a final year collection which was immediately snapped up by *Vogue* **stylist** Isabella Blow. His first collection during **London** Fashion Week introduced the bumster: a pair of **trousers** cut so low as to make **bottom** cleavage a reality. Many mainstream designers appropriated the idea and served up provocative views of bottoms with everything. He has also utilized the blood of crushed beetles, human **hair** and real locusts sealed in latex; his interest in military costume and traditional tailoring techniques has inspired a wide range of designers to follow suit. He is an innovator who, while favouring obvious shock tactics to display his ideas, encourages a debate which examines the underbelly of historical events and provides a launchpad for his highly innovative approach to design. His 'Highland Rape' collection attempted to depict the reality of a time in Scottish history during the seventeenth and eighteenth century when English forces quashed desire for self-rule. After his collection he was forced to issue a press release explaining his intentions. McQueen was recently quoted as saying, 'I don't know whether I can survive in fashion without murdering somebody; there are so many people who expect the obvious.'

men in skirts

Celebrated French designer **Jean-Paul Gaultier**, who designs for men and women, can frequently be seen wearing a kilt or a skirt, yet his attempts to introduce other men to masculine skirts, or even an asexual garment of **trousers** and skirt fused, have failed quite dramatically. But there are a few brave men who take issue with current rules for masculine dress: Jas Mann of Babylon

Zoo, comedian Eddie Izzard, the late Kurt Kobain of Nirvana, the late **Franco Moschino** and Boy George have all created their own spectacular styles by utilizing garments traditionally labelled as feminine. Popular reporting makes much of those men who attempt to cross dress. How can they be real men if they like women's clothes? Many journalists, male and female, end up questioning why a man would be attracted to women's clothes when there is such a vast selection of trousers, trousers and more trousers to choose from. The **uniform** of the weak, fragile and politically inferior should not be coveted by the ruling gender.

men's dress reform party In 1929 the Men's **Dress Reform**

Party campaigned for a certain amount of tolerance concerning their own strict dress codes. The main aim was to make comfort and hygiene a priority, doing away with the tight starched collars, **trousers** and boots for the summer at least. Shorts and sandals were suggested in what would have been an early unisex style. But little progress has been made when it comes to freedom from gender-specific clothing.

menswear A fast growing area of the fashion industry. For every

international fashion week devoted to women's fashions, there is an event offering the masculine equivalent. The big difference is popular media coverage. A scarcity of menswear reporting perpetuates the belief that guys are just not bothered. This is of course untrue; the 1990s mainstream menswear is boring and conservative, but **British** male **streetstyle** provides vivid contrast. Here is a space where young men dress to impress. A lavish mixture of peacock finery, the S&M studded leather and plastic chaos of punk, the comic book primaries of surfing and skating looks, all prove that masculine style can be exciting and energetic. Hip hop culture has made by far the biggest contribution to twentieth-century male dress styles, with many trends crossing over for mainstream consumption. The hooded **sportswear**, padded leather jackets, African colours and pendants have all become integrated with casual menswear styles.

Sadly for men, a big part of masculine culture is still about winning and controlling (it's a tough job but someone's got to run around being important). To be male is to be in charge and for those in office, the **uniform** must communicate the importance of the position. That the majority of western men cannot even bear to be seen (publicly at least) in bright coloured florals or soft decorated fabrics, is a testimony to masculine anxiety.

Mainstream menswear tells us a great deal about the expectation heaped upon the modern male. Textures and fabrics are chosen carefully to effect gravity or authority, and the ubiquitous suit strays little in design terms from standard cut. The association of sombre tailoring with professionalism and gravitas dates back to a time when middle-class merchants and traders (traditionally excluded from the pomp and finery of royal circles) began to acquire political power. As commerce flourished through Europe, the relevance of monarchy atrophied; royal finery and ostentation began to be regarded with ridicule and contempt. As a result, fashionable clothing and interest in it was deemed shallow and narcissistic. Eventually it was handed over as a feminine concern, and there it has stayed.

M is for Millinery. Award-winning milliner Phillip Treacy has his own show with full supermodel quota.

milan Known as the Birmingham of Italy, this city is home to Fiera Milano, a sprawling convention centre where Milanese designers show their wares. It's a city proud of its fashionable roots – tourists only have to ask for **Prada** or **Gucci** and Italian cab drivers will be half-way there before they've finished the sentence. There is less romance than **Paris** or **New York**, but Milan has considerable clout within the fashion community, not just because of designer highflyers, but as the home of

several giant and influential Italian labels, Genny, Complice, Maxmara, Sportmax, Marella and Callaghan being just a few. These are companies run by prestigious wholesalers who employ top names to create their ranges and hold packed catwalk shows. **British** designers have a strong presence: Scott Crolla currently designs for Callaghan, Keith Varty and Alan Cleaver design for the now independent Byblos line. Italian names like **Armani**, **Versace**, **Gigli** and **Moschino** have also enhanced the wares of these manufacturing houses. Other Milanese labels like Benetton, Fioruci and Hermes are forever engraved in our clothes-conscious minds. But there is a seamy side too. Some designers and their accountants have recently been under the spotlight for alleged bribery payments to tax inspectors, while the likes of Santo **Versace**, Gianfranco Ferre, and **Giorgio Armani** have been called to stand trial in corruption scandals that have rocked Italy and have the fashion world looking on in horror.

millinery
During **London** Fashion Week milliners provide a valuable service dressing heads and dispensing the finishing touches to the work of a **fashion designer**. When milliner Philip Treacy takes to the catwalk, however, he does it alone, with the full complement of **supermodels** specially flown in to model his impressive creations. His rare shows are amongst the hottest tickets in town. Millinery in Britain is once again a revered skill and colleges up and down the country include hat design as part of their curriculum.

In ancient times hat-wearing was intricately involved with ideas of modesty. A woman's **hair** was considered to be a powerful and magical substance; as Christianity took hold, it became a feminine duty to cover up. In the Middle Ages hat-wearing began to denote class and status. Rules sprang up to allow those with social rank to display it. Legislation like the English Statute of Apparel in 1360 even restricted the wives of yeomen to buying only English yarn, and stated that servants could not spend over twelve pence on a veil. The rich, however, could be as ostentatious as their money allowed. But by the 1400s hats of the nobility were so high that the Church objected. Women simply adjusted the height of their hats, and the millinery industry continued to flourish, felted wool being the most popular material at first, later replaced by beaver **fur** or rabbit. The use of a mercury solution and nitric acid to soften the animal fur so that it could be pelted resulted in the release of toxic mercury fumes. Workers suffered from hatters' shakes, and up until the 1860s mad hatters were causing the medical profession some concern as well as providing Lewis Carroll with inspiration. In the war years fashionable extravagance was curtailed, and hats have never fully been reinstated. After the fifties, with a new emphasis on social mobility and the vastly diminishing influence of the Church, hats as badges of authority lost currency. Add this to the emergence of a new generation of hairdressers like **Vidal Sassoon** who developed cutting techniques that emphasized freedom and fun, and the death of the hat was inevitable. But two decades later along came Lady Di. Most milliners agree that, combined with the early eighties new romantic style, Diana Spencer revived the hat. Today British milliners like Stephen Jones and Philip Treacy have gained international reputations as high fashion hats have enjoyed a revival. On the street black women in particular display an innovative mix of turbans, wraps and funky one-offs. The largest producer of European headwear is Kangol, headed by design director and couture milliner Graham Smith. But the continued expansion of the hat industry might be guaranteed by more than just stylistic concerns. In the late twentieth century, as sun-protective clothing becomes an imperative, headgear may reach new heights. Medical research suggests that both glaucoma and skin cancer could be reduced by the introduction of a shady brimmed hat.

m **105**

miyake, issey
Born in Hiroshima in 1938, Issey Miyake is a phenomenal force in the fashion world. His contribution began in 1970 when he established a design studio after completing apprenticeships for Guy Laroche and Givenchy. His fashion **shows** are awesome productions of contemporary design and presentation.

As he strives for a future vision where clothing is tactile, functional design in technologically advanced fabric, his presentations are noticeably bereft of wiggling girlies in saucy peek-a-boo styles. The music, a carefully harmonized fusion of synthesized whines and clanging sounds, provides an ethereal backdrop to a mural of colour, light and movement. His are the biggest and best shows, with standing ovations from an audience of normally jaded press and **fashion buyers**. After one such show, briefly overcome, the designer could not stop the tears as he bowed to the audience. He has been hailed as a genius, an artist and extraordinary visionary who embraces the future with rare curiosity and bravura. He and **textile designer** Makiko Minagawa develop innovative **synthetic** fabrics as a basis for his designs. Perhaps his delight in the future leads him further from the past, where he witnessed the deaths of most of his family after the atomic bomb desecrated his city. 'I remember,' he once said, 'but I thought I had better forget.' To date he has won awards from all over the world and never rests on his laurels. He is less popular with mainstream newspaper editors looking to print pictures of semi-naked models amongst their pages; but this is of little concern to the mighty one. His pleasure in his work, he says, 'Is to find new things, to have surprises. Negative things are good, they mean there is always something good to do. We must be curious. We must always go forward.'

model Unlike the super variety, *modellus ordinarium* is a hardier strain of men and women who do regular work and earn a regular wage. They can be seen smiling and smouldering from a whole range of mail order catalogues, mainstream **magazines** and trade brochures, in an endless sell-fest of products from thermal **underwear** to air hostess uniforms. Many models on the job carry a large bag of assorted **footwear**, underwear, tights and **hair** accessories, apply their own **make-up** in the toilets and keep their petrol receipts to claim against tax. Assignments are not always desirable, and less than favourite are the trade underwear shows attended by a range of men in suits looking to examine the merits of the latest push-up wired lycra and lace **bra** with matching bikini briefs. These models are rarely treated to **fantasy** photo shoots with celebrity **fashion photographers** in airy studios; their faces may not grace the front cover of anybody's magazine, and few have ever modelled in **Paris** or **Milan**. Most are happy, well-adjusted people able to earn a reasonable living and enjoy occasional travel. They are the reality of the modelling world, and one that is frequently neglected in favour of a more glamorous picture.

model agencies

There are many model agencies up and down the country which offer young women the chance to earn a living being someone else each working day. A good agency does not have to be based in the capital, although these tend to offer the most prestigious work (editorial with national and international **magazines**, television commercials, high-profile **advertising** campaigns and of course **catwalk** modelling for top **fashion designers**). Other agencies specialize in providing a look more suited to the commercial requirements of the mainstream market. The work is exactly the same, and includes photographic shoots for magazines, advertising campaigns, catalogue shoots abroad, catwalk modelling for trade and commercial shows and television. A good modelling agency, wherever it is based, will be a member of the Association of Model Agencies (AMA), and this must be checked out if you are thinking of joining. An agency will not take money from you for test shoots, or ask you to sign a contract. Apart from signing a standard AMA agreement, a new **model** is not required to enter into an individual contract (possibly packed with small print about wages, percentages and obligations) with any agency. Good agencies work with their models on the assumption that she or he is free to walk out at any time if unhappy or dissatisfied with agency conduct. A contract signed in haste with a less reputable agency may well lead to the model having to work on jobs she is unhappy about, as well as being powerless to leave. Agencies take a standard cut of 20 per cent from your wages. They also charge the client a 20 per cent handling fee. This is a separate fee, and does not have anything to do with your money. A good agency is there to negotiate your fee, regulate your jobs, your hours worked and regulate client requirements. They will screen out unreasonable requests, insist on breaks, bill the client and follow up the results so that you have tear sheets (the finished images as they appear in magazines), for your portfolio.

model agencies to avoid
Those that charge money for test shoots or compiling a portfolio. Those that charge money up-front for anything from shoots to headsheets. Those that require contracts to be signed. Those that charge large sums for training courses. Those that pressure you to lose weight. Those that do not put school work first. Those that do not belong to the AMA.

modelling
Getting started in this world requires a practical approach. First, you need to show yourself to a **model agency**. **Casting** days have become standard procedure for many agencies, when they invite hopefuls to turn up and be given an honest appraisal of their abilities. A skilled agent can tell in moments whether the applicant has the necessary bone structure, healthy skin and **hair**, attitude and ability to use their bodies and **faces** for a wide variety of clients. The height requirements are five feet eight inches for women and six feet for men. Sarah Doukas, owner and boss at Storm Model Agency, sees all applicants herself, and checks all holiday photographs sent. She usually responds to fifteen out of every hundred applicants, but eventually chooses less than five. Sixteen years or over is the preferred starting age, although in special cases agencies will liaise with schools, where younger **models** are involved; no agency should encourage novices to miss school. Models then undergo a period of tests with a variety of **fashion photographers** to build up portfolios. These sessions are free except for the cost of enlargement prints, as the photographer absorbs the rest of the cost.

Some agencies offer a basic training period where walking and grooming is observed. Consultations with hairdressers are usual, and your individual look is developed in accordance with your personality. At this stage lesser agencies may suggest that money spent on expensive photo shoots, so called 'classes' or 'headsheets', will enhance your career. They won't. A good agency will invest in its talent, and where money is needed, will advance against future earnings. Agents will then deduct small amounts out of wages over a period of time until the initial loan is cleared. When you are ready to start work you will be sent to castings, where client after client will assess whether your look is right for them. This can be a soul-destroying time, since some clients can be rude, personal and arrogant. Models are divided into categories. An A Girl is top of the range when it comes to status, earnings and desirability. She will be in great demand by international **magazines** for major fashion shoots. She will have done covers for all the most prestigious European glossies, including French and Italian *Vogue*, she has no doubt appeared in several high-profile **advertising** campaigns and television commercials, and features heavily on the catwalk. She will be a household name. A B Girl will be a household **face**, but not necessarily known by name. She too will have done covers, advertising campaigns and much fashion editorial. She will have big clients chasing her and can command $6–8,000 a day for catalogue work. C girls don't technically exist, but if the first two accreditations are not mentioned during conversation then clients know the status of the model they are discussing. For women, modelling careers are usually shortlived; few models are considered to be employable beyond their late twenties. IGM models recently created PR problems for themselves by clearing their books of sixty models who were over twenty-five. Some who have modelled return to the business as agents themselves, as did Lorraine Ashton and Sarah Doukas. Many return to the career options they had before they entered the modelling world.

moschino, franco

moschino, franco The last Moschino **show** I attended was a very emotional affair. The designer had died shortly before and the Milanese crowd of sleekly clad **fashion editors** were missing their joker. The finale garments worn by disco-dancing **models** having a party on the catwalk caused a stir, and, as the music pounded, members of the fashion élite joined in the spirit and danced around their **Prada** handbags.

A fitting memorial indeed. During his lifetime, Franco Moschino was universally admired for his comedy take on fashion and the fashion industry. His motto 'Who is to say what is good taste?' was apparent in everything he did. Fresh tomatoes were provided for the audience during his shows, and he dared them to let fly at styles they didn't like. The styling of the **clothes** he displayed were always adventurous and cheeky, models dressed head to toe in a riot of colour and pattern would sashay down the runway with the proverbial lightshade for a hat. Incorporated into his immaculately tailored designs were his now famous slogans 'Ready to Where' and 'Waist of Money'. One white shirt was designed to look like a straitjacket and stencilled on the back were the words 'For **fashion victims** only'. Gags were a part of everything he did.

Moschino was born in 1950, and he joined the Academy of Fine Arts when he left school. **Gianni Versace** spotted his talent and offered him illustration work. Upon entry to the fashion world, he soon turned his talents to design. In 1983 he launched his own company. 'My approach is contradiction,' he said. 'Why should I have to embrace the fashion business just because I work in it? I know I don't fit and the only reason I'm rich and famous is because the fashion system wanted me to be odd. The ones who really understand are the ones who can't afford it, the people out there on the street.'

moss, kate Since her discovery by Sarah Doukas of Storm **model agency** at an airport in 1988, the immaculate-cheekboned-one has risen to superstardom under the label super**waif**. She did not choose this title for herself, but with it she quickly gained entry to the titled world of the **supermodel** nobility. At just under five foot eight inches Kate's gaunt frame attracted an industry ready for change from the more womanly curves of Cindy and Claudia. Against a backdrop of grunge and anti-glamour Ms Moss, with her nonchalant lack of interest in grandeur and sophistication, began a love affair with the fashion media. In 1989 she appeared on the front cover of *The Face* and later from the freshly launched pages of *Harper's Bazaar*, where she established a presence that endeared her to American pundits. Meanwhile for **British** *Vogue* a set of photos saw her in common-or-garden tights and little else in a dingy bedsit, proving that the woman, not the **clothes** or the setting, were the main attraction. She has since become the **face** behind **Calvin Klein**'s fragrance Obsession, as well as starring in a whole host of international campaigns. She has dated film stars, published her own fully illustrated retrospective and received the British Fashion Personality of the Year.

She has also felt the full force of anger concerning the fashion industry's infatuation with thin adolescent women. Hoardings showing her pictures have been plastered with 'Feed Me' slogans, while those around her are resigned to reassuring us that she eats loads. Those who think the complaint is personal (and I have been charged with this) have missed the plot entirely. The issue here is not Kate's eating habits, but the eating habits of thousands and thousands of young women who want to be like Kate. Encouraged by her ordinary beginnings in Croydon, her girlish and easygoing demeanour and her shortness compared to other **models**, more youngsters than ever have fantasized a career in **modelling**. This they hope to achieve by acquiring by whatever means the skimpy statistics of the charming home-counties icon.

nearly no clothes In the fashion industry, quality newspapers find a more acceptable version of tabloid page-three girls. A **supermodel** in skimpy **clothes** is the perfect accompaniment to brighten up a page of crime statistics and home policy reviews.

new look Following the Second World War and a period of obscurity, Parisian **fashion designers** were anxious to reclaim the spotlight. In 1946, under the watchful eye of the Chambre Syndicale, designers created new modes of clothing. These were displayed on wire dummies and exhibited around the world as

N is for Nearly No Clothes. Long-suffering models are frequently required to strip off for designers and leap onto the catwalk to a fit of flash bulbs from an almost entirely male gathering of photographers.

part of an exhibition called *Théâtre de la Mode*. In 1947 the New Look was fully evolved and presented by **Christian Dior** to the world. The full skirt, requiring metres of fabric, drawn into a fitted waist and bodice and accessorized with **high heels** epitomized ideas of exaggerated femininity. Seen as decadent and vaguely debauched by **British** women – who had not only enjoyed freedom of functional dress while they worked in factories, but were still prevented from indulging fashionable whims by rationing – it was heavily featured in **magazines** with thrifty instructions on how to achieve a similar look. Gradually, women were convinced that the achievement of an eighteen-inch waist was much more attractive to any man than the fact that she and her sisters had run the country in his absence.

new york

This is the home of the Council of Fashion Designers of America and to some of the richest designers in the world. With an enormous buying public, the American fashion industry is geared towards mass consumption. **Clothes** tend to be safe and commercial, and for that reason, newer designers – like Todd Oldham, Isaac Mizrahi and Anna Sui – who offer a taste of adventure are popular with the American fashion press. Meanwhile, established names like **Ralph Lauren** and **Calvin Klein** are revered for the sheer scale of their businesses. Many of our own **fashion editors** have been lured to New York to inject a sense of **British** individuality into a bland publishing culture. New York didn't get going as a fashion capital until World War Two, when Europe had its mind on other things. Britain's trade links stayed open for essentials only, and rationing was implemented on all consumer goods. **Paris** was invaded by the Nazis, and many couturiers mothballed their companies rather than design for the wives of the army élite. In 1943 Fiorella La Guardia, mayor of New York, held the first ever Fashion Week and the CFDA was established. Journalists like Diana Vreeland advised on new collections and wore the work of the designers. American **retail** procedures have revolutionized the European approach; although the first department store was built in **Paris**, home-shopping, multi-complex shopping malls, designer discount villages and destination shopping stops are all inherited from across the water.

nostalgia One of the standards explored in fashion design, when inspiration is lacking. Designers may say they are reworking and re-presenting old styles with modern manufacturing techniques, and therein lies the excitement – but in truth the fashion industry looks back as often as it looks forward. This is done with the help of reassuring **clothes** and styles which symbolize particular images of femininity. It's no coincidence that the fifties are selected as the retro destination by so many popular middle-aged designers. They would have been small, helpless, and protected by a mother figure in **high heels**, floral prints and full skirts. If this didn't happen in reality for some, then at least the **fantasy** of perfumed matriarch can be resurrected and reassembled.

out Read any fashion magazine, and at some point or another, a fashion person in the know will be helpfully instructing those of us that aren't hip enough as to the correct procedures where trends in dressing, grooming or accessorizing are concerned. By strange coincidence, 'out' will be most of the clothing items we bought last year when they told us they were 'in'. If we are lucky, however, there will be another column with further instructions about what will be 'in' shortly.

When it comes to directions on style, however, I offer the words of fashion icon and ex-editor in chief of American *Vogue*, Diana Vreeland, who said, 'I don't go in for hideous fashion trends, and anyone who does is a fool.' Over and out!

O is for Ozbek. Naomi Campbell wears the designs of Rifat Ozbek.

outsize A standard industry term used to label the bodies of women who don't fit neatly into the dress sizes offered by manufacturers, which range between 10 and 16. Since the *majority* of **British** women are size 16 and over, this is ridiculous terminology, conveying not only the outdated understanding that the fashion world has of women's bodies (which are stronger and bigger than at any other time in history), but an implicit chastisement for daring to grow larger than the fashion industry is prepared to accept. Those actually in the business of providing **clothes** in sizes 16 and over have relabelled themselves somewhat, and now describe their merchandise in terms of plus sizes.

ozbek, rifat A **British** designer, who like so many others changed direction from architecture to fashion, Rifat Ozbek graduated from Central St Martin's School of Art in 1977. After working for Monsoon and completing military service in Turkey he began his own company in 1984. He is a confident creator and although known for his colour and exotica inspired by a childhood in Istanbul, his designs have a reality factor that reflects his own approach to life. In 1987 Future Ozbek – his cheaper range – was launched and in 1990, against all advice, he produced a pure white new age collection that inspired the fashion world. He is not a fanatic or materialistic and refuses like many of his contemporaries to colonialize the tastes of his fans by expanding into furnishings and other licensing deals. 'How can you improve on a white linen sheet?' he asks.

Those around him know that his drive is nourished by real life, not the need to be king of the heap and he is famous for his dislike of the post-show curtain call. During the backstage scrummage that follows he makes attempts at invisibility and once confided to me that the superficial questioning of journalists during **interviews** sent him spare. During one particular bout, he cut the interrogator short. 'I like it anyway,' he said and when pressed to continue with insights into the following autumn range he was equally concise: 'The same as spring with coats over.'

My kind of designer!

paris

Paris Fashion Week draws the biggest media crowd, and during a typical week up to one hundred **shows** take place. Many **British** big names like **John Galliano**, **Vivienne Westwood** and **Rifat Ozbek** are present. Paris has always been associated with high fashion, and history books show how French courts dictated styles and dress codes to the western world. French was the language of Europe's ruling class, and French customs and dress naturally became the currency for anyone seeking membership to a cultural élite. The entire field of wigmaking, dressmaking, **textile design** and general ornamentation was extremely developed as an industry in France by the 1700s. The first women designers and seamstresses emerged in the second half

P is for Platforms. Designer Vivienne Westwood's shoes have been known to reduce some models to quivering wrecks.

of the century, and the quality of craft was strictly governed by various guilds. Decadence and embellishment had reached such grand proportions by 1774 that doorways had to be extended to allow passage of the mountainous powdered **wigs** of the courtiers. The French Revolution in 1778 put an end to dressing up, and a wave of English styles – simple and plain – became popular. Then advances during the textile revolution meant that France once more entered into competition with the English for a share of the market. In 1801 Joseph Marie Jacquard produced the first successful loom, in which all the motions could be controlled by the weaver through the use of a complicated system of punch cards. Now *haute couture* emerged, as designers created a style which bore their name, and were protected by copyright instituted by the Chambre Syndicale de la Couture Française, founded in 1885. Ironically, however, it was Englishman **Charles Frederick Worth** who became the first and best known couturier.

performance fabrics
Nylon was an early 'performance fabric'; marketed as a 'wonderfibre', it took care of the ironing for us. Today fibre technology offers us microfibres which are sixty times finer than human **hair**, extremely strong yet soft to touch and machine washable. When tightly woven together, wind and water cannot penetrate. Comfort is another key factor in fabric development and the **sportswear** and outdoor market have proved to be rich areas for progress. Companies like ICI have recently introduced a double-layered knitted sports fabric called Aquator; this incorporates the nylon microfibre Tactel, which can draw sweat from the body and dispel it for speedy evaporation. Through a technique called microencapsulation, heat and light sensitive dyes can create micro-sized bubbles that connect to the fibre. These can then be filled with perfumed essences, heat-reactive liquid crystals or even bactericides for medical use.

platforms
When **Naomi Campbell** tripped elegantly down the catwalk and landed with a thump on her **bottom** a few seasons ago she made **modelling** history.

With her lean and lengthy limbs folded beneath her, and **feet** shod in outrageously high platform shoes, courtesy of **Vivienne Westwood**, she smiled gracefully as **fashion photographers** gleefully recorded the moment. She negotiated the terrible 'fear of falling' which all **models** have with ease. Platform shoes are the most curious of modernday **footwear** items. Reintroduced during the thirties as a platform sole of little more than half an inch in thickness, their historical roots date back as far as the early sixteenth century, when the chopine shoe was popular amongst Venetian women. Writers of the day have recorded heights of 'half a yard' as fashionable, and although extremely impractical (the nobler a woman was, the higher her platform soles) reformists of the day, including the church, made little comment. Needless to say, these women were effectively incapacitated and had to be accompanied and supported by their men or servants. Raised soles did owe something to function and practicality, however – in rural areas the patten, made of a shaped wood block a few inches in height, aided a foot already inside a shoe to walk across boggy paths without sinking in mud.

In the 1940s platform soles were made of wood and cork, owing to the shortage of leather. In the seventies platforms returned to accessorize an era lacking in grace and design finesse on every level. Vivienne Westwood, who uses historical inspiration for much of her work, reworks the idea of raised status through raised footwear for the nineties. In an environment where the shocking, the stimulating or just the downright stupid receive attention, Westwood's podium-like shoes became a device for raising her designs quite literally onto a pedestal; the clothes, the women and the design concepts are elevated to works of art in a gallery setting.

postwar fashion
After the Second World War a new breed of designer emerged. Male and business oriented, they took a different approach from their female predecessors. Instead of fitting the fabric to the body, ideas were sketched on paper. Designs became more daring and dramatic, with practical considerations

taking second place to striking effects. In an environment of post-war prosperity, empires were being built around ready to wear or **prêt à porter** designs for an idealized woman. As time went on, bodies became the adjustable element. Today we tailor our bodies to fit the **clothes**, in a complete reversal of function and form.

P is for *Prêt à Porter*. Some ready to wear clothes are not always intended to be wearable. Designer Thierry Mugler indulges his desire to turn Cindy Crawford into a baby doll cowgirl.

prada, miuccia

The current **uniform** of the fashion press is designed by Miuccia Prada, an Italian designer born from the family firm of Fratelli Prada, a maker of leather goods since 1913. A committed member of the Communist Party during and after her university years, Ms Prada resisted joining the family business until 1978, when she took over direction from her mother. Her early successes began life as items of luggage. Washable nylon backpacks were followed by hand-held bags. Functional and severe, the fabric is washable, flexible and tough. Her first ready to wear collection in 1989 was described as 'nothing on the hanger but extremely wearable'; minimal and devoid of fuss and clutter. With a design signature that borders on frumpy, she has managed to put an individual spin on nineties hard-edged femininity and ruthless practicality, and has initiated a mainstream fascination with **synthetic** fabric. Her younger and less expensive line is called Miu-Miu.

prediction agencies

High street companies like Gap, Marks & Spencer and the Burton Group use a fashion industry equivalent of a crystal ball in order to cater to customer need. For a price, a prediction agency will correlate trend books or mood boards, which spell out fabric types and silhouettes for the future, giving the store time to forward plan. This is essential, since fabric

production and factory time must be booked at least one year in advance. The agency studies style **cycles** and social and economic factors, as well as taking into account forthcoming world events like the looming millennium and even the soccer World Cup! Retailers also employ independent rapid-response companies who scrutinize the catwalks for key designs which work well in diluted form for the high street. These can be turned around in months, weeks, even days. Remember the summer of 1994, awash with Ecu, untreated fabrics, hessian weaves and unbleached cotton knits? That was the work of said prediction agencies, deducing a trend for downbeat dressing from a combined recession and heightened desire for a return to nature. But it's not all astrology and A-lines. Promostyle, a top **British** agency, lends its resources to Oxfam, offering a free insight into the future. By working ahead with small teams of producers from around the world, the charity empire can structure a **retail** strategy based on the same forecasting material as the high street giants.

prêt à porter The term *prêt à porter* means 'ready to wear' and describes a clothing revolution that took place shortly after the turn of the century. Right up to the 1900s, dressing up in fine fabrics, with beading and embroidery styled in the latest fashions was only possible for society women who patronized *haute couture* designers, and for middle-class women who employed personal dressmakers. While the Parisian élite visited the salons of **Charles Frederick Worth**, or Paul Poiret for personal fittings, those with their own dressmakers would expect news of the latest **Paris** fashions so that they might copy The Look. Clothes were elaborate, complicated and full of fabric. With the advent of the **Dress Reform** Code, as well as design pioneers like **Coco Chanel**, came the simpler lines that required less cloth and expertise. Those who could not afford dressmakers' prices were able to run-up their own creations from home. *Vogue* or Butterick offered paper patterns of the latest styles, and women's **magazines** advertised their own special offer patterns. Now clothesmaking for fashionable occasions would become a feminine hobby, and women could use their sewing skills to dress themselves fashionably for the first time. The arrival of improved machinery in Britain in the 1920s enabled wholesalers to cut and copy fashionable outfits for mass production. As ready-made **clothes** began to appear in department stores, Paris couturiers, not slow to recognize a business opportunity when it was slapping them about the **face**, descended from their lofty perches of expensive fittings and society clients to oblige a more mainstream market. **Chanel**, Patou and Lelong were amongst the first designers to open shops selling passers-by clothes which were *prêt à porter*, and **British** designers like Edward Molyneux soon followed suit.

public relations
All fashion designers have PRs. Some use established independents in the field and others have an inhouse operation. The job of a public relations officer is to interest the press in the activities of clients. **Fashion shoots**, launches and lavish **shows** are considered to be the best way to attract writers, who then make a story for magazine or newspaper editorial. **British** PR Lynne Franks was the pioneer in this field; she came to prominence in the eighties, when she started garnering publicity for her husband, designer Paul Howie, who owned a shop in Covent Garden. Her profile grew as she successfully marketed a variety of new and established designer names at a time when the world's fashion media focused on **London** designers. She eventually broadened her client list to include celebrities and household products, but always with an eye on trendsetting and product performance in the style department. Ms Franks later sold her company and is now much involved in the all-female radio empire Viva. She still serves as a role model for many who are attracted to PR, and of course provided the inspiration behind Jennifer Saunders' character in *Absolutely Fabulous*. Novice PRs can learn initial marketing and fashion communications skills on a variety of college courses up and down the country, but the cut and thrust of the industry needs to be sampled firsthand during a work experience placement. A confident telephone manner is an absolute must. The ability to organize a champagne and tofu brunch in a canalside warehouse studio, bedecked with lilies, clubland cross-dressers and assorted celebrities also helps.

quant, mary Born in 1934 in **London**, Mary Quant OBE is the name most people associate with the sixties. She produced bright simple coordinated **clothes** that epitomized young **British** fashion, and popularized the mini skirt, coloured tights, skinny ribs and even **underwear** as outerwear. She, like most in her day, started with relatively little experience. After graduating from Goldsmith's College of Art in London, she opened her first shop, Bazaar, in the King's Road in 1955 with Alexander Plunket Greene, who was later to become her husband. Alexander, who had inherited £5,000, encouraged an architecture student to give the shop a face-lift, but both neglected to request planning permission. It was only after a lot of

Q is for Queues. Designer Jean-Paul Gaultier can whip up queuing frenzies with ease. His dramatic and humorous take on fashion and clothes means that tickets are hot property.

tears from all three of them in the presence of an inspector with a warrant, that they were allowed to keep it as it was. The label took off quickly, and her low-priced fashions were an instant success. The fabrics were bought from Harrods at **retail** prices, because said shop had a policy of allowing accounts to run for one year before demanding payment. In an equally eccentric move Mary refused to deal with American chainstore tycoon JC Penney, who owned 1,765 stores across the USA, because she didn't believe his credentials.

Together with Alexander, an instinctive marketing and sales man, Mary forged an identity. Linking up with **Vidal Sassoon**, who was himself receiving rave reviews for his new haircutting techniques, Mary had him cut the **hair** of all her **models**. A look was born that to this day epitomizes sixties style. It was time to expand further. Money was tight, but America with its huge market, was beckoning. So sandwiches were duly packed for the (then 36-hour) flight and after four days of visiting fashion **magazines** and top stores, the orders came rolling in. JC Penney revealed himself to be genuine, and a ten-year relationship was begun. Her **make-up** range featured the daisy she'd always drawn on designs for fun, and in 1965 this was patented and designed with black and silver packaging to present a range of make-up which was to take its place in history. Waterproof mascara, previously pooh-poohed by chemists, was a roaring success, as were false eyelashes, sold in strips to be cut to size. There was also a skincare range of vitamin tablets, as well as **lipsticks** and eyeshadows like crayons. She was the first designer to explore the potential of design in other areas. A shoe collection with the tights attached followed, so that the whole lot could be tossed in the washing machine; later a move into interiors introduced fashion into the home for the first time. Designer wallpaper, bedlinen and carpets for mass market consumption were pioneering products of their time. Mary Quant now sells all over the world. She has two hundred shops in Japan alone, and has plans to launch in Korea. Mary attributes her success to her ability to have fun; she attended ballet classes at six, but really wanted to be a tap dancer:

'When I look at my drawings of happy rhythmic figures, I see a tap dancer enjoying life, just as I have.'

queues

All **fashion editors** queue to get into **shows**. This is easily the least favourite moment for those who live and breathe **glamour**. And for those of us who just want to get the job done they are a wind-up. In a world where the latest fashions and newest ideas make riveting news flashes, queueing systems are chaotic and antiquated, sometimes even hazardous. In the past **fashion designers** have been accused of planting frenzied mobs at the front of the building in order to whip up 'entry desperation'. This looks good on film and many press crews shoot the crowd scenes as part of the report. What really happens is that those without tickets arrive early and congregate at the doors, making it impossible for others to penetrate the throng. Fashion editors have to make their way through the crowd like everyone else. One year esteemed fashion doyenne Liz Tilberis of **British** *Vogue* was punched in the face while her designer **footwear**, already covered in mud, also took a beating as she fought to enter **Jean-Paul Gaultier**'s tent in the middle of a field.

rabanne, paco

While in some countries his name has become a generic term for aftershave, Rabanne made his name in the sixties for his inventive approach to shift dresses. Made from plastic, metal discs and chains, he used pliers instead of needles and thread to construct a metallic patchwork of geometric shapes. He also designed dresses from crinkled paper, aluminium and jersey towelling seamed with scotch tape. His fame rocketed further when he entered the **fragrance industry** in partnership with Parfums Antonio Puig of Barcelona, and marketed his sweet smell of success for all to wear. This is all a far cry from his early days, born in 1934 in the Basque country, the son of socialist parents. He lost

R is for Recycled. Most mainstream designers flirt with the concept of recycling; in reality this nerdy patchwork ensemble from Comme des Garçons may well have been created to make a seasonal statement only.

his father in the Spanish Civil War and fled with his mother to **Paris**. His mother, who had been the chief seamstress for the great Spanish couturier Balenciaga, found work in his Paris division, but the two were soon lying low during the German occupation of France. Paco later attended the Ecole des Beaux Arts as a student of architecture, but soon, with his mother's connections began selling bold plastic buttons to Balenciaga, **Dior** and Givenchy. Today his empire is vast and his name known throughout the world. He has taken to writing bestsellers and exploring his past lives. He was once a prophet and acquaintance of Christ, as well as a prostitute to the King of France. In 1990 he revealed that he had arrived on earth from a distant planet. He says that fame means little to him and his huge salary is donated to charity. While most fashion hacks continue to ponder the meaning of fashion, he already has an answer: 'Fashion is a characterization of humanity. It is the external appearance of an epoch. Our civilization has made image all important. The best known woman on earth is Claudia Schiffer – and what is she? She's a coat hanger!' Ah Paco, I couldn't have put it better myself.

recruitment Since the advent of fashion on television, more and more people have considered a career in fashion and textiles or allied fields. Britain has approximately one hundred art colleges, many of them offering a fashion or textile based course, or marketing and communications courses. Courses can be broken down into various categories: BA three-year courses; BA sandwich courses of four years (a sandwich year is spent in industry or work placement); and HND technical courses of two years. A one-year foundation course at a local college is frequently advised where the enrolment of a BA is concerned. On the down side, classrooms are overcrowded and tutors are overworked. On the plus side, potential entrants are called 'clients' and are treated with a certain amount of business hospitality. Many graduating students find work abroad, and in every top designer house **British** accents can be heard. But many do not find work, and the system of teaching fashion design in particular is criticized for producing too many lead singers and not enough band members. Broadening the range of skills taught would ensure that other areas of industry are serviced. A recent British Fashion Council survey of students showed that 60 per cent were working in the UK industry within six months of graduation, and a further 11 per cent were employed by fashion companies abroad.

You do not, however, have to attend college in order to succeed, some extremely creative self-taught designers ply their trade from market stalls, offering personally made and individual items. Other disciplines, like fashion writing and fashion photography, offer opportunities for those who have a creative streak, and many people in this world did not necessarily embark on a college course beforehand.

recycled

When Helen Storey made the headlines during one **London** Fashion Week by showing her charity-bought old **clothes** redesigned into new, she was received with a certain amount of bewilderment. In fact she was leading the way for the future of fashion, and, although she infused her message with a liberal dose of humour, she was very serious. The fashion industry is not the most **environmentally aware** of trades, but there is a growing culture of creative salvage. Many designers are now working directly with old clothes, producing new designs by recovering the undamaged parts and incorporating them into a resourceful patchwork process; Scrap Scrap and Conscious Earthwear are just two such companies (both run by women). Recycled fibres are also used; companies buy rags directly from charity organizations or factories, break them down by passing them through spiked rollers, disentangle the fibres and then twist them into new thread.

Synchilla is a type of recycled fabric made from plastic bottles! The bottles are broken into tiny flakes and melted before being woven into a fibre that has similar qualities to wool, but is far lighter with a much shorter drying time. It is also extremely soft and has excellent heat-retaining properties, which means it lends itself to outerwear and **sportswear**. Patagonia is a Californian company specializing in Synchilla and other garments made from PCR (Post Consumer Recycled waste). We can all recycle, and Oxfam have led the way in providing their own label clothing made from cast-offs, as well as offering clothes – for the purists amongst us – that are quite literally recycled from one wardrobe to another.

retail

In every high street there is a variety of chainstores, or 'multiples' as the trade likes to call them. These shops have revolutionized the way we are able to buy fashion, as fashion is truly democratized. Many of the designers who work for such stores have impeccable credentials, having been through art colleges and owning their own businesses. Fashion director Jasmin Yusef, for example, has reinvented the Warehouse chain.

Department stores are a French invention; among the first were Grand Halles in 1853, and Bon Marché, established around 1860. Two early stores in England were Kendal Milne and Faulkener, in Manchester (1836), and Bainbridge in Newcastle (1845). Then in the period 1855–75 came Dickens and Jones, Swann and Edgar, and Peter Jones. Meanwhile Macey's of New York, set to become one of the most famous of all stores, opened in 1860.

Probably the best known chainstore in Britain today is Marks and Spencer, started in Leeds as a marketstall in 1884 by Lithuanian Michael Marks. He was joined by Tom Spencer in 1894. They offered all goods at one penny, and by 1900 had twelve shops and twenty-four marketstalls. The stalls and shops were called Original Penny Bazaars. Mr Spencer died in 1905, and two years later Mr Marks followed, leaving his son Simon to run the growing company with partner Israel Sieff. In 1926 the company went public, and today there are 285 stores in the UK and 628 globally. Known as the Knicker Nirvana of the world, the St Michael brand shifted 85 million pairs in Britain alone. In an attempt to enhance the clothing image of the company, they have implemented a design led policy which has earned them a **British** Fashion Award. It also led to a *World in Action* programme in which swimwear designer Liza Bruce accused them of copying her work.

rhodes, zandra
One of the very few **textile designers** to have achieved the status of household name, an honour usually reserved for Parisian or Milanese couturiers, Ms Rhodes was born in Chatham in 1940 and studied textile printing and lithography at Medway College of Art. When she graduated from the Royal College of Art in 1966, young designers were busy upturning the stuffy dress codes of the fifties. Her designs — instantly recognizable handpainted or handscreened soft chiffons and silks with beading, quilting or intricate embroidery — became very popular. In the eighties she hit the headlines with her Punkcouture range of elegantly slashed and draped designs held together with golden safety pins. Her shows regularly feature **models** with elaborate **make-up** designs using sequins and jewels on their faces. Besides operating many franchising businesses in Japan, America and India, including interior fabrics and wallpaper designs, Zandra Rhodes has examples of her highly individual textile designs featured in museums all over the world. She has won numerous awards and holds many doctorates from prestigious colleges. She remains recognizable by her shock of red **hair**, always worn on top of her head, and her colourful and painterly application of **make-up**. Although a grand dame of fashion (she's even had a *This is your Life* programme dedicated to her), Ms Rhodes is wonderfully modest and approachable.

sander, jil Besides **Karl Lagerfeld**, she is the only German designer to have huge international presence. Ms Sander is known as 'the queen of design without decoration' and produces **clothes** of impeccable simplicity. This designer combines sensuality with authority to effect a stunning vision of austere grace. Her design ideology is as finely tuned as her business sense and she controls a million dollar empire; she recently sold a third of her company on the stock market, for a personal profit of $56 million. Brought up by her mother, she studied **textile design** and later became **fashion editor** of the popular *Petra* **magazine**. She produced her first collection in 1973 and sees her designs as ones which can merely frame and

S is for Streetstyle. Fashion relies on streetstyle for inspiration. Karl Lagerfeld adapted the oversized denim uniform worn by hip hop pundits for Chanel and even commissioned a rap soundtrack by TLC to accompany his designs down the runway.

accentuate the woman inside. The antithesis then of the dominant approach in fashion design, where the body not the wearer is the star player. Jil clarifies her vision further: 'I like to see women looking cool, I like to see their personality.' More please!

saint laurent, yves

Born in Algeria in 1936, Yves Saint Laurent is rated as the fashion genius of the late twentieth century. Extremely perceptive to change, he was the first couturier to see the revolution of the sixties in the direction of casualness and fun, and his Pop Art couture collection during this time made an enormous impact. At twenty-one, after winning first prize in a competition sponsored by the Wool Secretariat, he was employed by **Christian Dior**. When Dior died four years later, Saint Laurent took over, and proceeded to arouse controversy with his adventurous designs influenced by modern **streetstyles**. In 1960 his modernization of the House of Dior was cut short as he was called to serve in the Algerian war. Upon his return, after illness, he found he had been replaced by Marc Bohan. In 1962 he promptly opened his own house with business partner Pierre Berge, and from the start he was adored by the fashion press. He cut a dashing figure, always immaculately suited with his signature dark-rimmed spectacles and luxurious mane of **hair**, and soon his initials came to adorn everything to do with fashion. He sits at the head of gigantic cosmetic empires, (although a high percentage is actually owned by Charles of the Ritz). A charming and dignified man, he occasionally grants **interviews**, but cannot disguise the appearance of one who would rather be somewhere else. His health has given cause for concern for some time, and it has been suggested that he is only wheeled out to titillate interest. When I have interviewed him, his vagueness has certainly been apparent. Those around him are extremely protective. 'Yves was born with a nervous breakdown,' Pierre Berge is reputed to have said.

sassoon, vidal

Credited as the hairdresser who gave birth to a cutting technique which rebelled against previous starched and dressed styles, Sassoon completely redesigned heads for the sixties. He combined hip popularity with keen marketing skills to powerful effect. Today he is approached with reverence, while his cutting techniques are taught to thousands of students every year in teaching salons all over the world. In classic fashion style Vidal Sassoon's beginnings are humble. Born in 1928, his mother dreamt he might one day become a hairdresser, and the fourteen-year-old Vidal agreed to visit Cohen's Beauty and Barber shop in **London**'s East End to discuss an apprenticeship. The young Eastender's hope of learning under Adolph Cohen (fondly known as the Professor) seemed dashed when he learned a fee of £100 was required. However, his impeccable manners stood him in good stead, because his graceful acceptance of this disappointing news prompted the Professor to offer him an apprenticeship on the spot for nothing. By 1954 Sassoon had opened his first salon, and in 1958, shortly after opening in Bond Street, *Hairdressers' Journal* declared 'Vidal Sassoon is the big name in hairdressing this week and might be even bigger in years to come.' His most famous cuts were the bob in 1963, and the five point cut in 1964. His friend and muse **Mary Quant** was receiving much interest for her clothes designs, and together they fashioned a look that appeared on the front covers of *Vogue* **magazine** all over the world.

During the seventies Sassoon began the now well-trodden path of developing his own hair care range, which he sold in a lucrative deal. Vidal has since concentrated efforts on international presentation of his craft with seminars and **shows**. He is the author of various books and boasts numerous international television engagements. In the early eighties he hosted his own syndicated show *Your New Day* in the US. He now adds corporate might to the **British** fashion industry, by sponsoring the twice-yearly designer collections, and has considerable presence worldwide. In the Far East and former iron curtain countries young women can be found shaking their locks in imitation of the model in the now-famous ads as they 'Wash and Go' about their daily business.

schiaparelli, elsa Born in Rome in 1890, Elsa studied philosophy and music. After her husband left her and her child — an extremely difficult situation in those times — she moved to **Paris**. When a sweater she had designed for her own use was bought by a Paris store, she turned to fashion design to make a living. She began making **clothes** in the twenties and soon amassed a huge following for her designs, which flouted previous standards for femininity. She liked to shock and amuse, and she worked with famous artists of the day including Salvador Dali and Jean Cocteau. In 1933 she introduced the influential pagoda sleeve or Egyptian look, which lasted over a decade. She used tweed to make eveningwear, put padlocks on suits, dyed newly invented plastic zips the same colour as her fabric and featured them in a decorative way, and showed phosphorescent brooches and buttons. She even produced handbags that lit up or played tunes when opened. A shoe hat, designed with Dali, and a clear plastic necklace crawling with bugs are amongst the most memorable designs she created. She also produced an early range of **make-up**, including **lipsticks** in jarring colours like deep purple and bluish pinks, which shocked sedate sensibilities. Her signature colour was shocking pink, which was also the name she gave to her fragrance (sold in dressmaker dummy bottles). Sadly she did not regain her position as fashion leader after the Second World War. She died in 1973, leaving behind a reminder to all that fashion was not to be taken seriously. **Vivienne Westwood** cites Schiaparelli as a mentor, and the work of the late **Franco Moschino** also owed much to her approach.

show Formerly sedate affairs in dainty salon environments where mannequins with numbers on their wrists paraded stiffly, today's fashion show has become an all-singing all-dancing event. With international press crews jostling for space and tents seating many hundreds of buyers, press and celebrities, showtime has become much more than a preview of clothing. With popular icons placed carefully in the front rows, ready to talk about their latest film, current single or newest lover, the usual complement of superbeauties on stage, and the designer of the moment on standby in a 'will-she-won't-she-grant-us-an-interview' situation, the collections are readymade news events for a whole host of programme-makers.

In order to secure coverage, the pressure is on for each designer to better their last show. In Europe this usually manifests itself in an opulent demonstration of wealth; lavish set design, giveaway presents on the first few rows of seats, and a highly technical lighting and sound presentation accompanying the full complement of supers. The likes of **Karl Lagerfeld** sell **Chanel** designs to the world media in just these ways. **British** designers, however, without a huge budget at their disposal, have turned to less obvious ways of making a statement. Car parks, warehouses and underground tunnels are popular, cheaper venues, with live DJs and spooky ambience. Theatres, restaurants and stately homes have also provided sympathetic venues. Red or Dead came up with the unlikely concept of a floating catwalk in a swimming pool, while **Alexander McQueen** showed a recent collection in his local church. Protesters braved the cold March wind to furnish the fashion press with ancient homilies condemning vanity, while security staff could be heard inside frantically ordering smokers to stop defiling God's holy quarters. Most fashion writers, however, acknowledge only one God, and she is Suzy Menkes of the *International Herald Tribune*.

slimming
Few industries are as successful as the slimming industry when it comes to selling consumers nothing and charging vast sums for the privilege. Dieting is a female occupation, with a vast industry of services and products specifically geared to encouraging women to take up less space. Even without the aid of dynamic ad campaigns or exciting products, this multi-million pound industry continues to grow, feeding like a parasite on the bodies and minds of healthy women. Highly-processed tasteless foods, books, **magazines**, even drugs – these are some of the products we are encouraged to gorge on. And of course, the

fashion industry stands close by, providing encouragement and reward; only once the body is reduced may the owner enjoy the latest styles. In the US there are hundreds of fat-burning products, but when the Center for Disease Control analysed the contents of 300 such products they found dubious substances such as insect hormone, of no known use in humans. Side-effects not so well promoted are high blood pressure, heart palpitations, nerve damage, muscle pain and stroke. The accessory market, which had refrained from offering slimming tips of any kind, could bear it no longer. Acu-slim earrings, small magnets which apply pressure to a recognized acupuncture point in the earlobe, aim to reduce hunger pangs by increasing the level of endorphins in the brain.

spinning This is the process of making thread or yarn from natural or **synthetic** fibres. According to the Toulouse Guild Statutes of Finishers and Weavers, written in 1279, all spinning was undertaken by women. In fourteenth-century Barcelona, women worked at looms in the wool industry, frequently owning their own businesses and employing others. Spinning was a fine and noble occupation, and was understood to be the domain of women. Women who spun were spinsters.

When this word first entered the English language in Langland's *Piers Plowman* in 1362, 'spinster' had come to signify 'woman alone'. In *Brewer's Dictionary*, we are told that our forefathers reckoned no young woman fit to be a wife until she had spun for herself a set of body, table and bed linen. Now spinsterhood had become an undesirable state, or at least a temporary predicament until someone would rectify the situation with an offer of marriage. In the **fairy-tales** and stories handed down to us today, **witches** always live on their own, and so too do spinsters. Cultural understanding of both words down the centuries is of a dried-up hag. In a few hundred years, the history of the spinster as powerful member of society, manufacturer and business-woman was buried. In *Webster's Dictionary* today, spinster is described 'an unmarried woman and an old maid', with absolutely no mention of her previous greatness.

sportswear

Sport has had a big influence on popular designs for men, women and children in the 1990s. Designers like Anna Sui and **Katharine Hamnett** designed whole collections around ideas of fitness and athleticism. Those of us who wear trainers, **clothes** with go faster stripes, tracksuits or just the company logo on **t-shirts** are saying we're ready for action. Notions of speed and agility are explored through lycra cycling shorts and athletics vests, while certain urban tribes base their **uniform** around the sport they most enjoy. Surfing culture contributes washed-out vests, mangled sunbleached hair, leather or cotton friendship bracelets and reef sandals, as well as music and language. In fact those rubberized sandals have inspired a wave of styles from competing outdoor companies, confident that young **British** men will at last step confidently out (socks compulsory) in the knowledge that these sandals are sporty and blokey. Young women in old school pumps, nerdy nylon sweatpants and anoraks are the vanguard of latest sports looks.

Just one hundred years ago sportswear for women was non-existent. For tennis, for example, the correct attire was a long skirt with a bustle, a shirt and stiff linen collar, tie, straw hat and petersham belt. Women had to play modified versions of some sports because their clothes inhibited movements. But the invention of the bicycle – impossible to ride in huge petticoats – brought about change. **Bloomers**, ridiculed in previous decades, added a sense of practicality if an accident was to reveal 'unmentionables' to members of the public. Once out of heavy clothes, women did not intend to return. One woman who singlehandedly did away with 'corsets on court' was Suzanne Lenglen, who won the women's tennis final at Wimbledon from 1919 to 1926. Her skill as a player attracted almost as much attention as her clothes did. Wearing a one-piece loose fitting dress designed by Jean Patou, and over the knee socks, she upturned dress codes that required a woman to play tennis with her skirts trailing in the mud.

stockings

Today leg fashions are a market in themselves. Lycra has allowed hosiery to take on the appearance of a second skin, and designers have exploited this with brightly coloured prints, psychedelic styles and even animal prints which appear to be actually on the skin. In the twentieth century, women's legs are on show. When nylons were launched in 1940 (Nylon fibre was introduced by the Du Pont company of Delaware in 1938) women were working towards the war effort, performing heavy manual tasks traditionally the territory of men. With new-found confidence, money in their pockets and financial independence for a while at least, an urgent need for female workers to confirm their femininity surfaced. Legware became a high-profile concern. Nylons became highly desirable and synonymous with lovely legs. A shortage of luxury goods made nylons hard to come by, so some ingenious damsels painted the trademark seam down their legs in the absence of the real thing.

S is for Streetstyle. During the eighties, clubland produced its own dress codes and in Britain, post-punk streetstyle uniforms for women were photographed for magazines all over the world. Clubland hostess Scarlett was amongst the most celebrated.

Somehow those stockings and suspenders, worn as part of a rigid elastic girdle to hold everything in place, have come to represent an era. In the post-war fifties stockings were staple items, and **underwear** with cone-like **bras**, and rigid **corsetry** was unyielding and uncomfortable; but in the sixties, as women were literally bursting out of tight restrictive clothing and questioning the inhibited lifestyles that hemmed them in, stockings and suspenders were quickly replaced by no-nonsense – and slightly unappealing – tights.

streetstyle

Britain is the streetstyle capital of the world. **Jean-Paul Gaultier** regularly fuses this peculiarly **British** style with his design ideas while

Karl Lagerfeld spices up **Chanel** offerings with current streetstyle trends. British fashion is widely acknowledged as having a creative streetstyle edge and this is part of the reason why amongst the fashion industry giants, **Milan**, **Paris** and **New York**, we remain an attractive destination for press and buyers. Fresh ideas are what **London** Fashion Week offers foreign traders. In fact, one of the world's best known designers has her roots in streetstyle. **Vivienne Westwood** created a **uniform** for punk that launched her career as the most enigmatic designer this side of Chanel.

Fashion and streetstyle are two different things, however, and it is often the former that relies on the latter for inspiration. Traditionally streetstyle has been a display ground for masculine creativity (with British **menswear** prohibiting expressions of vanity or interest in appearance), female uniforms have either utilized what was currently in fashion or emulated the male styles of the Rockers, Mods and Skinheads. With Punk, things changed and a feminine look that took issue with traditional western ideas of **beauty** emerged. **Make-up** was used to create body art or African tribal decoration and influenced mainstream fashion to such an extent that cosmetics giants manufactured jarring colours and hair products to create the streetstyle look, while designers like **Zandra Rhodes** had a field day. Black-led streetstyles have also made phenomenal impact and today Caucasian teenagers are inspired by the language, politics and music of Hip Hop culture as well as the uniform.

stylists

stylists Fashion **designers** rely on stylists to accessorize their **clothes** for the catwalk. A good stylist will work with the designer to divide the **show** into themes, then, using music, props, accessories and **hair** and **make-up** changes, the **show** is presented like a film without a script. The stylist has considerable power, and exercises choice concerning **models**, hair and make-up teams. In the early eighties **fashion editor** Amanda Grieves and **John Galliano** forged a partnership that resulted in a magnificent collection of memorable moments on the catwalk, and Amanda — now Lady Harlech — works with him at Givenchy. Meanwhile ex-*Elle* fashion director Debbie Mason has helped revitalize the face of Ghost, placing them at the forefront of **British** fashion. Where portrayal and setting of the product is concerned, a stylist is a designer's right-hand woman. Those who also work for glossy cutting-edge **magazines** have extreme power in influencing mainstream trends. Caroline Baker, who began her career on the influential *Nova* magazine of the sixties, pioneered many trends in womenswear and began a subtle advertising dialogue with the early Benetton ads. The late Ray Petri evoked cinematic imagery of men and **menswear** that disregarded previous publishing requirements like having to see as much of the clothes as possible. He was instrumental in establishing a new approach, creating a mood and concentrating on the personality of the model. Working with cutting-edge photographers and eighties style magazines like *The Face*, he blurred imagery, placed models far in the background and concentrated on scenery, or used close-ups of faces with the merest suggestion of clothes.

Pop performers acknowledge the power of the right look, and will work with a stylist who will often go shopping with them to advise on stage and photographic clothes. Judy Blame, who has also used the pseudonym Fred Poodle, began his career within the pages of *i-D* magazine and is now much sought after. Björk, Neneh Cherry and Massive Attack are just a few who have benefited from his attention. The fashion industry will always have a need for image-makers and this is a skill that doesn't have to be learned at college. Essential here are contacts within the designer world (although many stylists begin on a clubland level); then designer clothes, combined with market finds and personal items, the services of a budding model, photographer and make-up and hair artists, provide the finished image.

supermodels
More famous than any Hollywood leading lady, these women are known by their first names alone and don't even have scripts to learn. Such is their pull that **fashion designers** have been falling over themselves to book this clutch of modernday goddesses to adorn their catwalk **shows** and reel in the

column inches. The faces of Linda, Christy, Naomi and Kate peer out from **magazine** covers, TV ads and billboard campaigns. They host their own shows, star in films, offer fitness advice, dominate gossip columns, and have their pick of male icons in the film and pop world. Their success is based on a **face** that fits western standards of absolute **beauty**, a body that conforms to height and weight requirements, and an ability to yield chameleon-like to the demands of a whole host of assorted image-makers. Behind these women is an army of specialists in the **fantasy**-making world. **Make-up** artists, hairdressers, agents, bookers, **fashion editors**, art directors, **fashion photographers**, advertisers and designers are all involved in the business of creating the look, the image, the moment and the million-dollar face! Supermodels (the term itself is not new – it was coined by Clyde Matthew Dessner, owner of a small American model agency in the 1940s) do earn supersalaries. With a business-like grip on their own marketability, models instruct their agents to negotiate a fee of hundreds of thousands of dollars as an original contract, and then build in various extras like appearance fees and separate photo usage fee (some even include clauses in their contract to control the geographical placement of their image). With agents all over Europe and America, it has been possible to buy someone like **Christy Turlington** over and over again as her image appears on the front cover of a dozen **magazines** simultaneously. It is worth noting that this is one of the few jobs in which women can out-earn men. There are varying reports about earnings, but all agree that these women have banked millions, with some estimates putting Claudia's earnings in the £12 million bracket.

At the height of the supermodel love affair, it was **Linda Evangelista** who offered the now immortal words 'We don't get out of bed for less than £10,000.' It has been reported many times since that those words were taken out of context. Linda was simply acknowledging her own and her supersisters' power, but it backfired royally and the mainstream media swung round for a critical view at the antics of the fashion world. When a French magazine requested an interview, Linda didn't see it coming and allegedly asked for £10,000 with a 20 per cent service fee thrown in for good measure. According to American fashion writer Michael Gross, the paper replied publicly to Ms Evangelista's wage requirements by pointing out how many Somali people could be fed for such an amount. Magazines who had booked these models when they were just starting out were being refused **fashion shoots**, and **fashion designers**, irritated at dealing with frequently late and sometimes moody beauties, began to question the cost. American designer Todd Oldham put his foot down and refused to hire a particular siren – reputedly **Naomi Campbell** – quoting the 'No asshole' clause. Finally Italian designer Laura Biaggotti sacked Ms Campbell on the spot and donated her £12,000 fee to charity after the Streatham-born super arrived at the show too late to be prepared.

But why has the industry had enough? With Linda Evangelista in her thirties and some other supers in their late twenties, time itself has decided on an ending. **Model agencies** are clapping their hands with glee as a whole load of new faces – or girls as the industry likes to call them – are ready and willing. Billed as fresh and vital (as opposed to tired and jaded?) these teenagers, some as young as fifteen, are all too ready to fill the space.

swimsuit
In 1907 Australian swimming champion Annette Kellerman was arrested on a beach for indecent exposure. Ms Kellerman's crime was to wear a

functional one-piece bodystocking which allowed for movement in the water and freedom from the heavy waterlogged garments women had been forced to wear. **Coco Chanel** was one of the first designers to cater for women needing some slack, but costumes known as bathing suits were still only designed for light bathing activities like paddling and strolling. In 1925 Fred Cole stopped making Hollywood B movies and went back to his family's **underwear** business, where he quickly became the darling of the liberated flappers by lowering the back of his knitted swimsuits to allow sun worshippers to cultivate tans to show off in their daring backless dresses.

In the thirties, fitness and efficiency became attractive qualities and swimming and swimwear enjoyed considerable popularity. In 1941 the Varga calendar offered a variety of pin-ups in the swimsuit designs of the day made of rubberized yarn. Before she became Marilyn Monroe, Norma Jean Baker was prone to a spot of swimwear modelling. By the fifties swimwear was about enhancing feminine attributes, and contained built-in **bras** and stomach-flattening girdles. Innovative developments in foundation garments later allowed for the Curvelle breast cup, a stiff-looking cone that 'remembered its shape under water'. The advent of Lycra in 1958 gave swimsuits a second skin appearance, and designers like **Mary Quant** and Courreges offered highly stylized designs. In 1964 Austrian designer Rudi Gernreich offered the topless suit; it didn't take off, but in its wake daring Europeans could be seen rolling down their swimsuits to create similar effects while sunbathing with the utmost dedication. The last thirty years have seen a variety of designs, but the main focus has been on fitness and performance. Swimwear designer Liza Bruce has concentrated on athleticism, using bold colours and streamlined designs. Our modernday attention is firmly focused on thighs and buttocks, as designs cut high above the hipbone can effect a vision of long-limbed grace.

synthetic Synthetic fabrics are rated highly by modern designers for their 100 per cent unnatural abilities: they have 'memories' that allow a return to the original shape, they can effect exaggerated textures, change colour, protect from damaging ultraviolet rays, they may even be able to emit fragrances. Teflon-coated textiles do not absorb liquids, and so stains could become a thing of the past. Whole outfits could be fused together without the need for seams and then melted down to be recycled. Some experts are investigating fabrics that can receive sound; others have already marketed fashionable clothes that give 80 per cent protection against nuclear radiation. Fifty years ago this was unimaginable. Early fibres were launched under the umbrella of 'easy care fabrics'. Billed as modern and therefore desirable, Nylon, derived from benzene extracted from coal (today known as Polyamide), was invented by American chemical giant Du Pont in 1938. In 1941 Polyester came from two oil derivatives, and others like Acrylic soon followed. During **laundering** they did discolour and also made wearers hot and sticky. By the seventies, fabrics permitted the wearer to sweat in the heat but stay dry in the wet. Then came Lycra (originally invented in the late fifties) that could bend like a second skin with the wearer. These malleable and accommodating materials have sometimes fallen out of favour, as during the oil crisis of 1973 when raw materials became hard to source and 'synthetic' became a dirty word.

Today, as the fashion industry continues its current adoration of computer-aided design and technology – helped no doubt by the work of masters like **Issey Miyake** – synthetic fabrics look set to stay. But rest assured that many are currently being developed to contribute to an environmentally friendly role.

teenager Messages from the fashion industry tell of an effortless adolescent existence, and young women can confuse the **fantasy** they are offered with the reality of their own lives. But glossy photographs of happy, pretty teenage girls who seem accustomed to the designer world of beautiful **clothes**, fast cars and handsome men do not tell the truth. These seemingly confident young women often have self-esteem problems of their own. But it is easy to feel like an outsider because the media world of fashion **magazines**, beauty **advertising** and the diet

T is for T-shirts. A perfect site for statements. From top left clockwise: Linda Evangelista and her Twiggy T; on the runway of Red or Dead, a model states the obvious; Katharine Hamnett's makes a plea for worldwide peace back in '84; and Nadja Auermann wears her own personalized item for American designer Todd Oldham.

industry presents such a distorted view. Most **eating disorders** begin during adolescence, when worries about identity surface. For many young women the unattractive image they believe they have and the low self-worth they then acquire are hard to shift as they journey into womanhood.

textile design
The popularity of the psychedelic Lycra designs of Pucci in the late eighties and nineties heralded a mainstream fashion for bold print, which sparked off a variety of successful relationships between textile designers (the unsung heroes of the fashion industry) and **fashion designers**. Often unaccredited, textile designers may work with fashion designers months before a show to create a spectacular look based on one-off vivid prints on individual garments, or create a selection of signature designs for the fashion designer to weave in and out of his or her work. Sue Clowes produced bold handpainted symbols and shapes for Boy George, while Hilde Smith worked with Bodymap to create memorable computer-graphics inspired designs. Luivan Rivas Sanches, a **London**-based Venezuelan, enjoyed a partnership with **John Galliano**. Later The Cloth, a company featuring four textile designers from the Royal College of Art – launched in the mid eighties – pioneered the idea of textile design as an artful and high-profile discipline. There are many clothing designers who specialize in fusing the developments of fabric technology with their own sartorial vision. Georgina Godley made an impact in the late eighties with her exploration of form and silhouette which resulted in a collection where the **clothes** had a life of their own. **Issey Miyake** has pioneered the use of extravagant and technologically advanced fabrics which have refocused interest on the design of the garment, rather than the body. **Christian Lacroix** uses decorative embroidery, weaving and print to effect a vision of opulent splendour.

There are many textile designers who are stars in their own right, **Zandra Rhodes** being amongst the best known. Georgina Von Etzdorf's traditional florals, arty textures and patterning (influenced by Paul Klee) have earned her a strong following in Italy. Sue Timney and Graham Fowler of Timney Fowler, who specialize in monotone classical architectural prints, have built an empire from their shop in the King's Road which deals with fabrics, soft furnishings and ceramics.

trousers The introduction of the bicycle in the 1890s thankfully

created an environment that allowed women to adopt a **uniform** for the purpose of riding a bike. Years before, suffragettes had tried to do away with the compulsory heavy skirts and rigid **corsetry**, but were unsuccessful with their **dress reform**. Now the time was right for the introduction of the split skirt: a huge balloon-like pair of three-quarter length breeches. Trousers themselves took longer to become standard female attire, since men held on to an item which, they felt, required masculine credentials. But in the 1920s, as women in America and Europe were demanding the right to vote, slacks and even shorts for sporting activities began to appear. In an attempt by men to gain some control over the situation, rules about where trousers could be worn – and more to the point, where they could not – were hastily invented. Many still exist today. Certain work places insist on skirts during office hours, some schools will not allow slacks to replace the outdated school skirt, and some public buildings insist on a no-trouser rule. In her wonderful book *The Language of Clothes*, Alison Lurie gives the example of the Frick Collection Library in **New York**, where visitors who are ignorant of the no-trouser rule are given an ancient and unattractive skirt to change into if access is still desired.

t-shirt When top Parisian couturier **Christian Lacroix** included the printed

faces of Helena, Kate and the rest of the superearners on **t-shirts** amongst his collection, he was confirming the versatility of this mighty garment. T-shirts, originally an item of **underwear** for American men, are indispensable twentieth century staples – multipurpose, adaptable and comfortable. In lightweight cotton or **synthetic** mixes they are the antithesis of the heavy-layered and restrictive clothing of the past. In the *T-Shirt Book*, John Gordon and Alice Hiller document the history of the t-shirt, noting that in South Africa in 1986 Cape Police used 'emergency' regulations to ban the wearing of t-shirts with slogans. **Katharine Hamnett**, two years earlier, had met Margaret Thatcher with '58% Don't Want Pershing' emblazoned across her chest. Her statement sold the idea of fusing fashion and politics; fortunately, however, no one had threatened Katharine with ten years in prison. Other **fashion designers** meanwhile were busy selling themselves as opposed to politics, and the cult of the designer t-shirt allowed fashion fans to wear the name of a favourite frock-maker on their chest. Today sports branding is the most desirable motif for chests, and is worn at clubland and mainstream level. The t-shirt gives us all a site for displaying our thoughts: Naomi wears one that says '**models** suck'.

turlington, christy
Born in 1969 in Oakland, California, the daughter of a Pan Am pilot and ex-stewardess, Christy Turlington was spotted at fourteen by local photographer Dennie Cody. At the time she had curly **hair** and braces, and having watched enough television to have an authoritative adolescent opinion on the **modelling** world, was reluctant to enter. But she did. For a while, she kept her career secret from her schoolmates, signed up with Ford Models and went to **New York**. During the summer of 1985, aged sixteen, she did the rounds. *Vogue* **magazine**, last on the list was interested and booked her for one week. In spring 1988, when Christy was modelling for **Calvin Klein**, she received a proposal of sorts. She was to be the woman for his new fragrance. She hastily signed a contract that was to pay $3 million dollars for eighty days' work over a period of four years. After realizing that she had agreed to various career restraints such as being forbidden to work with any photographer other than Bruce Weber, or appear in any clothes other than Calvin Klein's, she terminated her contract after eighteen months. In 1992 she signed the highest contract price ever for a model at that time, worth more than $2 million for twelve days' work for mass-market **make-up** giants Maybelline. Other appearances have netted $25,000 per show, as when **Gianni Versace** paid her to

model in his show alone. With a reputation for being the nicest of them all, Christy's relaxed yet hardworking approach has earned her many admirers. But she is no soft touch and, it is reported, kicked one photographer and slapped him round the **face**. His crime: taking a topless picture of her with a concealed camera and publishing it in the *Daily Express*. She was justifiably applauded for this by a bevy of beauties sick to death of being gawped at by photographers with little lenses. Her ability to represent both ends of the commercial spectrum, from the most sophisticated to the most ordinary (like her Special K ads in America), has earned her a respect and affection that eludes others. When she has finished modelling Christy Turlington plans a return to college and a future career in writing.

underwear It was **Vivienne Westwood** who first displayed the **bra** over hooded tops as part of her Buffalo collection. Madonna, who up until this point had been jigging about in footless tights and rara skirts, embraced the look to make it her own. Meanwhile, **Jean-Paul Gaultier** and **Dolce & Gabbana** both have a thing about their mother's **corsetry**. This is nothing new, today women's underwear holds a considerable amount of fascination for the average man. For that reason, bra **advertising** appeals to male voyeurs as well as female consumers.

For many years, underwear was little more than a full and long chemise, tucked into drawers held up by a drawstring. **Stockings** would be fastened to the bottom of

U is for Underwear. Intimate apparel is often reworked as overwear. Dolce & Gabbana specialize in saucy offerings.

these. From the 1830s onwards petticoats, corset covers and camisoles were added: then came stiffened underskirts, quickly replaced by the crinoline petticoat or cage, made from flexible steel circles and lightweight fabric. Towards the end of the 1800s the bustle required a different style of petticoat, heavily frilled at the back and with 'sweepers' to collect dirt, protecting the dress from damage. For women and little girls who wore the full corsetry and petticoat quota from the age of eleven, the whole business of getting dressed was time-consuming and tiring. In the 1880s Dr Jaeger, professor of physiology at the University of Stuttgart, extolled the virtues of health and hygiene in the wearing of wool next to the skin, because wool was porous and would help skin breathe. From this point onwards, underwear began shrinking in size. As various fabrics like elastic (originally invented in 1830) became popular, the desire to control and contain the female body re-surfaced. Huge slabs of elasticated material incarcerated many women during the fifties. Conical bras and girdles or roll-ons offered wearers the elegance and firmness they were told their natural shape lacked.

In 1958 Lycra was invented by Du Pont of Delaware. It had stretch and recovery powers far superior to elastic, with the added bonus of being three times as powerful as rubber. Now boneless, seamless corsets, seamless bras and bodystockings enjoyed popularity. Some men like to collect these delicate, lacy, personal items of clothing, possibly because the possession of it allows for the **fantasy** of closeness with femininity. Women on the other hand are unimpressed with the masculine equivalent: this no doubt has everything to do with the amount of tired paisley pants or boxershorts that have languished in the communal laundrybasket, waiting for the woman of the house to clean them. 'For men obsessed with women's underwear,' declared Charlotte Perkins Gilman in 1916, 'a course of washing, ironing and mending is recommended.'

uniforms Women have strict uniforms, primarily for the use of defining gender: fastenings that close on the right, along with colourful and flimsy designs using tactile or sensual 'feel me' fabrics. These are introduced to little girls the moment they are born. Pink lacy rompersuits are followed by pastel dresses with cuddly 'stroke me' animal motifs. Light colours unable to disguise dirt force parents into prohibiting muddy or grimy activities. Little boys of course can get as dirty as they like in darker colours with action motifs like 'get out of my way' cars and sportsmen. Adolescents rely on their clothes to display association with a peer group and use an agreed dress code to signal their embrace of a football team or youth culture movement. As we grow older the uniform becomes more specific to gender. Feminine styles are body hugging, revealing and flamboyant, while men, from city banker to corporate executive, unanimously favour the ubiquitous suit, modelled on a traditional fighting uniform. With streamlined silhouettes, small crests, piping and top collar folded back to make a lapel, modernday **menswear** is little more than a depiction of civilian infantry.

Fashion editors have their own uniform. The matt black sleekness, black sunglasses and coordinated accessories favoured by these doyennes have earned wearers the title of 'style mafiosa'.

versace, gianni Born in Italy in 1946, Versace began training at his mother's side. Mrs Versace had a dressmaking business, Mr Versace was a coal merchant. At 25 Gianni Versace left the studio of his mother and began work as a fashion designer for Callaghan, Complice, and Genny, all top Italian companies. In 1978 the first Versace collection hit the catwalks. He earned his first major award, L'occhio d'Oro, for the best womenswear of the season in 1982. In 1989 he opened Atelier Versace, a couture workshop which has clients spending millions in one go, and in the same year he presented Versus, a line for younger clients. He also offers Versace Jeans Couture, Instante, childrenswear and Versatile, a larger sizes range.

V is for Versace. Claudia Schiffer as the Barbie Doll Darling in strappy Versace Special.

Today he offers his design ideas in a variety of forms, including his homeline signature which includes tiles, vases and carpets as well as the usual bed, table and bath linen. But he is still best known for his lavish, stylized tailoring. Of his skill there is no doubt, but he is a tits and arse merchant who loves to pour his supers into cleavage-hugging, slinky styles. Naturally the world's press love this too, and he has been perplexed in the past by the accusation of misogynist. He has justified his approach as being that of a designer who makes big dresses for big egos. He is in the business of freeing women's egos: 'I try,' he told a reporter, 'to help women be liberated.' His strategy clearly pleases plenty of women, and his wealth is estimated at £400 million. From his studio in **Milan** he works from a computer library containing millions of volumes on art and fashion. His brother Santo controls the purse strings, and sister Donatella, eleven years younger than him, is the driving force behind his Versus line, and developed Blonde, the latest perfume. Versace's logo, a Medusa head, adorns everything, even the cushions in his own **show** venue. His invitations are amongst the most coveted in the fashion world, as there's the extra attraction of a frontrow full of pop and cinema stars. He even runs an informal **clothes** hire service for celebrity big nights out.

victorian fashion
A century ago, fashionable presentation was an essential skill to acquire, and the most prestigious wife for a successful, sober suited businessman was one who concentrated on displaying his wealth tastefully and fashionably about her person. The crinoline, one of history's most ludicrous design concepts, reached the height of popularity during the 1850s and epitomizes the modernday, derisory term **fashion victim** with extreme accuracy. During this time, the clothes of the wealthier classes revealed much about their place in society. As Elizabeth Rouse explains in *Understanding Fashion*:

> Fashionable dress created a barrier between the fragile lady and the
> possible dangers of society! The crinoline kept a physical distance

between a lady and her companions, as did gloves which were never removed in public even to shake hands. The bonnets and veils worn until 1869 sheltered her from unpleasant sights and unwelcome gazes.

These women effectively managed themselves like living, breathing, museum statues. With little exercise and restrictive clothing (**corsetry**, popular for shaping tiny waists, displaced internal organs and restricted breathing), it's no wonder many Victorian women became sickly and fragile, often falling ill at the slightest germ. Suffering, sickliness and ill health were seen as part of a woman's lot, and evidence of true exquisiteness. A romantic vision of women as gentle, delicate creatures, not able to overtax themselves, served the masculine culture of the day and men enjoyed the role of protector and lord and master. Since financial security could only be procured through marriage, many women were forced to exhibit the approved feminine characteristics in order to attract a mate. Still today we aspire to such outdated descriptions of femininity to do the same. Waifishness, delicateness and petiteness are all favoured states constantly sold to us by the fashion industry, and especially the diet industry, as a way to attract a man.

waif When new model **Kate Moss** was marketed, amidst a fanfare of glossy fashion editorial, she was billed as the superwaif – a newer and more exciting **face** and body to die for. The marketing angle was her thinner-than-thin body. Headlines praised her delicacy and fragility, recalling the impact of another featherweight, almost thirty years before, who had gone by the name of Twiggy.

westwood, vivienne Born Isabel Swire, in Glossop, Derbyshire, in 1941, Vivienne Westwood is the most influential female designer this side of **Coco Chanel**. She is copied the world over, and has spectacularly reworked current

W is for Wigs. In Europe in the 1770s, women excelled in the art of the giant bouffant and slept in chairs so as not to disturb the arrangement. Karl Lagerfeld recreates the look for Nadja Auermann.

clothing silhouettes by re-presenting costumes of bygone days. 'I am the only designer who is bored with the twentieth century,' she once proclaimed. Ms Westwood didn't start out with a particular desire to enter the fashion world. After moving with her family to **London** aged seventeen, she began work in a factory, intending to save for a secretarial course. She changed her mind, and eventually trained as a primary school teacher, securing a teaching post in Willesden. During this time, she married Derek Westwood and birthed the first of two sons. After a period of single parenthood and part-time work in a jewellery store to make ends meet, she met Malcolm McLaren, a student six years her junior, and entered into a business partnership that spawned one of the most dynamic youth movements in the twentieth century – punk. Malcolm managed the Sex Pistols while Vivienne kitted out a whole generation of vacant ones with her designs from her shop at 430 King's Road.

Although she had begun designing in 1971, it wasn't until 1981 that she presented her first collection of pirate-inspired asymmetrical **t-shirts**, petti-drawers, breeches and baggy-round-the-ankle boots from the Pillar Hall at Olympia. In 1982 she chose to show collections in **Paris**, and has since moved between the two, gathering acclaim and ridicule in equal measures. Her inspiration may come from a celebrated fascination with historical costume, but her insights find favour in the present. The silhouette she introduced in the mid-eighties, based on the crinoline, challenged and overthrew a popular style for women based on imitation masculinity. The power-dressing statement of the time – square shoulders and slim hips, introduced by French designer Thierry Mugler – was nothing more than a wannabe exercise, and Vivienne threw it out. By placing emphasis on the feminine form, with its roundness and power-base at the hips and stomach, she offered a visual statement of strength and creativity.

With a design ideology that reflects how she feels about herself, she told *i-D Magazine* 'I've never thought it powerful to be a second-rate man. Femininity is stronger, and I don't understand why people keep plugging away at this boring asexual body. At my age I'd rather have a bit of flab.' Ms Westwood, however, while undermining certain long held ideas on the female body and its display, also offers a contradictory approach, with her own liberty bodice and high-rise **platform** shoes which both pay homage to a femininity restrained by awkward and restrictive apparel. Mainstream consumers have found her hard to understand, and have not been helped by media portrayal of Vivienne as a batty eccentric. 'Way out Westwood' declare banner headlines, while Vivienne does her best to state her case: 'I'm not crazy, I'm not wealthy and I'm not a mess.' In a culture that does not value ageing women, she stands defiant in her rocking-horse wedge shoes, Lycra bodysuit and fig leaf.

wet look Introduced in the early sixties by **Mary Quant**, wet look, a Nylon fabric with a shiny easily torn wafer thin top layer, was an early instance of mainstream adaptation of **fetish** materials. Billed as 'risky' and 'daring' by fashion writers of the day, now ordinary consumers could dabble with fetish clothing, which up until this point had existed separately from high fashion. In fact, since the early 1800s, when Scottish chemist Charles Mackintosh developed rubber, these seemingly saucy second skin fabrics have struggled for acceptance. By the 1870s a **London** newspaper was **advertising** night shirts and caps in Mackintosh cloth, but carefully attributing medicinal properties to the clothing, claiming that the induced perspiration cured rheumatism. More than a century later, when I wore a rubber vest, leather chaps and shiny Lycra long black evening gloves, the BBC received a peeved letter from a very 'respectable' male viewer who did not think my attire suitable for teatime viewing. Of course now that **Versace** and many others have exhibited their own rather more raunchy high fashion fetish wear offerings, in a bid to investigate new territory, and sophisticated **magazines** have extolled the virtues of latex, wet look, rubber and PVC, resistance to these clammy fabrics has all but vaporized.

wigs Many designers have used wigs to accentuate their designs on the catwalk; the exaggerated styles make for dramatic photographic opportunities, and fulfil an aesthetic brief by framing and reducing the **face** of the female wearer to create a look of delicacy. Early wigs were made from the real **hair** of poor women or slaves, but it was not until King Louis XIII of France lost his hair through illness that the wig became popular for everyone. Wigmaking was a lucrative business, and in **Paris** alone during the mid 1600s records show the existence of 850 wigmakers. Wigs at this point were worn enthusiastically by both men and women, who used the mountainous structures, made from a variety of ingredients like silk, mohair and goat hair, to add inches to their height. The fashion soon spread to England, but it was denounced as 'devilish' by the Church, possibly still battling with ancient teachings that attribute magical powers to hair. In France the end of the wig came suddenly when working-class French revolutionaries revolted against the aristocracy. The elaborate powdered wigs worn by the French ruling-classes not only became a dead giveaway for those trying to escape the guillotine, but also a despised symbol of wealth and excess. Back in Britain in 1795 Prime Minister William Pitt the Younger introduced a tax of a guinea a year on the use of hair powder, and strenuously enforced it with fines. One professional group was exempted, and still today lawyers, barristers and judges perch a wiry thatch upon their heads before attending to business.

witches In her early career **Cindy Crawford** was frequently told she would not be booked with a mole above her lip, and advisors suggested covering it up or airbrushing it out of final prints. Even those of us who do not appear in glossy **magazines** are under pressure to justify the presence of moles when a plethora of **beauty** clinics can render us blemish free. During the Middle Ages millions of European women were burned as witches by a Christian Church frightened of female sexuality and knowledge and intent on stamping out any last traces of the matriarchal religions that preceded the patriarchal Christianity. In order to justify the torture and death of ordinary female doctors, midwives and spinners, the witchkillers looked for 'witches' marks'. Warts, moles, an insensitive spot which did not bleed when pricked, birthmarks, pimples, pockmarks, cysts, liverspots, sores or blemishes of any kind were seen as incriminating evidence. So were dissimilar eyes, pale blue eyes, or red **hair** (especially combined with freckles). Some women were even imprisoned because of an insect bite or an ulcer. The letter of the law may change, but the spirit lingers on. Ask Cindy Crawford.

worth, charles frederick Born in 1825 in Lincolnshire, Charles Frederick Worth was the founder of a house that became the world's longest running fashion dynasty. He was the first to present **clothes** on live mannequins, using his French wife as a model, and was amongst the first to set up an *haute couture* business, which opened in 1858. An excellent businessman, he was also the first to sell designs to be copied in England and America. He began work at the age of twelve in a **London** draper's shop, followed by an apprenticeship at the haberdasher's Swann and Edgar's. Shortly after, he convinced a store to open a department of made-up designs, a revolutionary move in itself. In 1845 he went to **Paris** and started the House of Worth. He quickly rose to become a top Parisian couturier, kitting-out the likes of Sarah Bernhardt and the Empress Eugenie. Unable to draw, he sketched his ideas on pre-drawn figures. He is said to have abolished the crinoline and invented a princess style dress with tailored touches in an early appropriation of masculine tailoring for women. When he died in 1895, his son Gaston took over the business with his brother Jean-Phillipe. Gaston was the first president of the Chambre Syndicale de la Haute Couture. The business continued to pass into the hands of grandsons and great grandsons until 1954, when it was sold to Paquin, another longstanding French couture house. Parfums Worth continues today, with Je Reviens the most famous fragrance.

zeitgeist The people, the **glamour**, the **clothes**, the **beauty**. The fashion

world and all its darlings make exciting news. But what is it about this world, which

offers to package our lives to perfumed perfection, that so attracts?

Fashion has always been *the* sign of the times, and in the twentieth century, the

fashion industry has become a powerful economic and cultural force, visiting

poorer or lesser economically developed countries with its promise of industry and

sophisticated aesthetics manifesto: the appearance of femininity especially is

moulded to suit Caucasian tastes and European desires. As we export our designers

and their vision into Asia, (the latest site for a make-over), along go our **advertising**

campaigns, and our rigid ideas around gender, **age**, race and **beauty**.